Film Actresses

Volume 16

Loretta Young

Documentary study

Part 1

ISBN-13 : 978-1502944696

ISBN-10 : 1502944693

Dtp
and
graphic design

Iacob Adrian

Author statement

The actors and actresses are the the bricks .

The cast and crew are the plaster .

They stand on the foundation created by
producers and writers and directors .

All these people creates the great palace
of the art of film .

Iacob Adrian - 2013

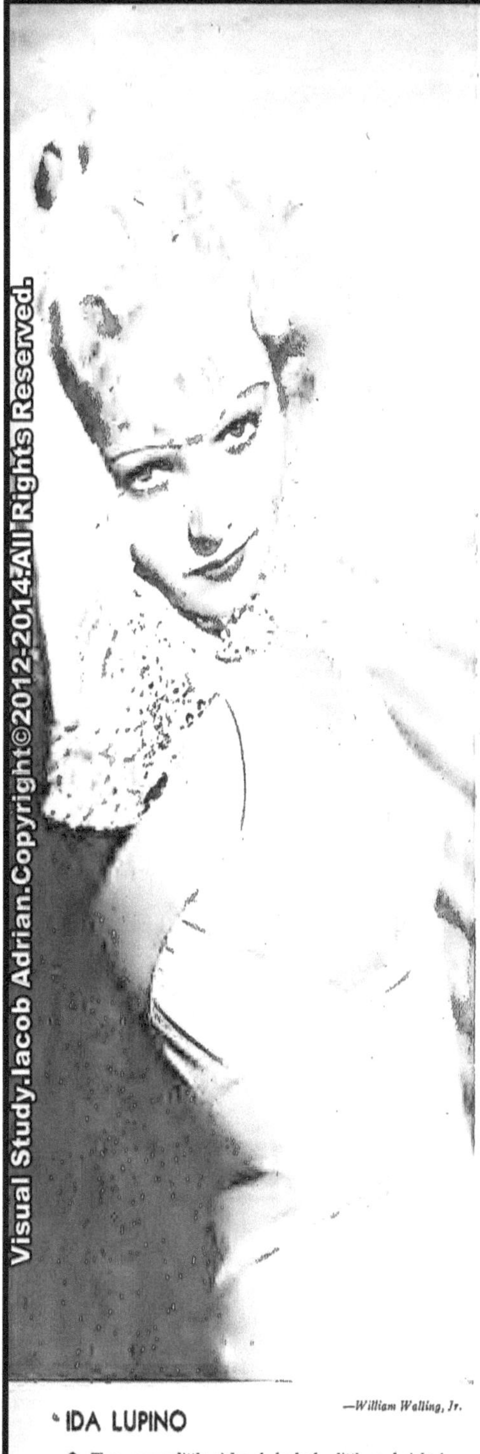

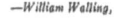

—*William Walling, Jr.*

—*Kenneth Alexander*

▪ IDA LUPINO

● There was a little girl and she had a little curl right in the middle of her forehead—and her conquest of male Hollywood was quite complete. Ida is to be seen currently in Paramount's *Come on Marines*

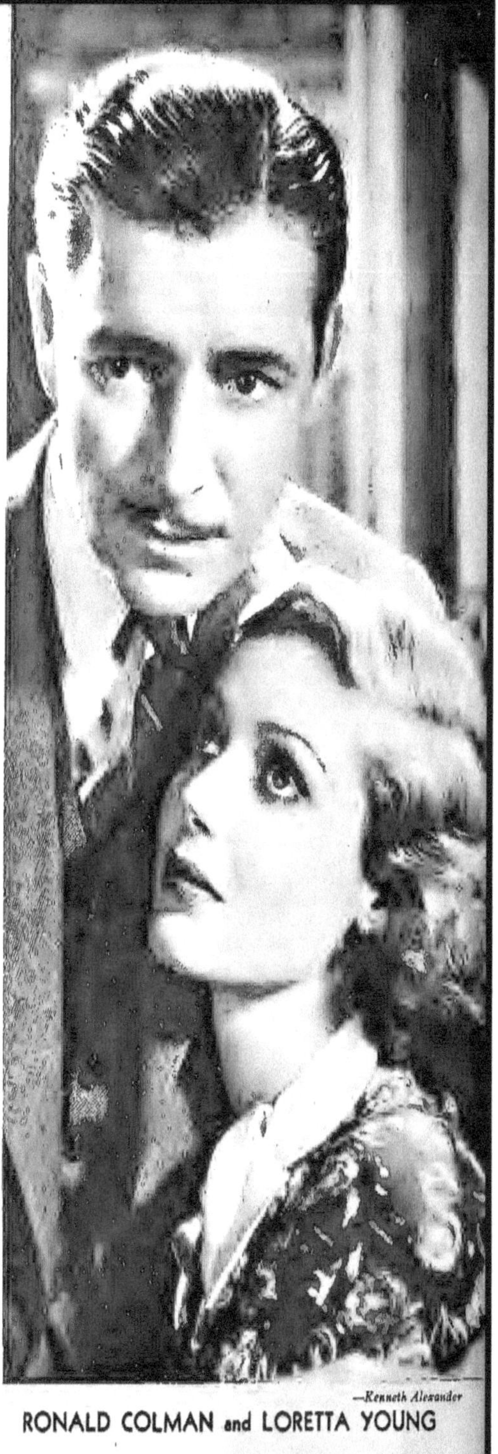

RONALD COLMAN and LORETTA YOUNG

● Fresh from his extended vacation abroad, Ronald Colman is engaged in filming a sequel to one of his greatest successes, *Bulldog Drummond*. Loretta Young plays opposite him in Twentieth Century's *Bulldog Drummond Strikes Back*

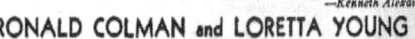

young man, all in a private car heading for New York while the old mystery standbys transpire — murders, lights flashing on and off, eerie voices and the rest of them. The comedy is continual and enjoyable.

His Greatest Gamble
● ● ● This is Richard Dix as his fans —particularly the feminine ones—like to see him. A gambler reckless in his profession and sentimental in his love for his infant daughter, whom he has kidnaped from his divorced wife, lands in prison accused of a woman's murder, and later escapes to restore happiness to his daughter, Dorothy Wilson, now grown to young womanhood. Edith Fellows, Bruce Cabot and Erin O'Brien-Moore are excellent support.

She Learned About Sailors
● ● ● A light, fast-stepping comedy which is bound to please. Alice Faye and Lew Ayres do fine work as the night club entertainer and the sailor whose romance almost goes on the rocks. It's a swaggering tale of the navy ashore in an oriental port and its interest is increased by the antics of Frank Mitchell and Jack Durant. Not a dull moment.

Bachelor Bait
● ● ● A pleasing little comedy with plenty of laughs and human interest. The story concerns the building of a successful matrimonial bureau by Stuart Erwin, an idealist, and Skeets Gallagher, a more crafty and practical soul. The entire cast—including Pert Kelton and Rochelle Hudson—have exceptional opportunities to display their talents.

Here Comes the Groom
● ● ● The presence of Jack Haley and Mary Boland makes this a bright and entertaining comedy. Haley gets himself wanted by the police to please his girl friend, but is captured by an heiress, in whose home the girl friend later turns up as a servant. The cast includes Isabel Jewell, Neil Hamilton, Sidney Toler and Patricia Ellis.

Our Daily Bread
● ● ● ● A beautifully written and expertly directed picture depicting the heart-rending struggle of a young couple faced by the problems of the depression. It will strike home to the hearts of millions who have gone through the same struggle, and it is reminiscent of King Vidor's other epic, *The Crowd*. Tom Keene and Karen Morley turn in exceptional performances. See it by all means.

The Most Precious Thing in Life
● ● Jean Arthur appears in what is for her a new type of rôle, one in which she is called upon to portray both youth and age, and she comes through with telling effect. Donald Cook also shines in a dual-age part and Richard Cromwell and Anita Louise are excellent. The story is set against a college background and concerns a father's attempt to break up his son's romance, and the heroic struggles of the mother—long since divorced and working as a servant at the college—to thwart his plan and prevent another heartbreak like the one she suffered when Family and Tradition were allowed to smash love.

Here Comes The Navy
● ● ● Some of these days somebody is going to discover James Cagney is an actor. In spite of the fact this is the same sort of stuff Jimmie has been doing since he pushed a grapefruit in Joan Blondell's face it's a wow. Plenty of thrills, romance, comedy, Pat O'Brien, Gloria Stuart, Frank McHugh and NAVY.

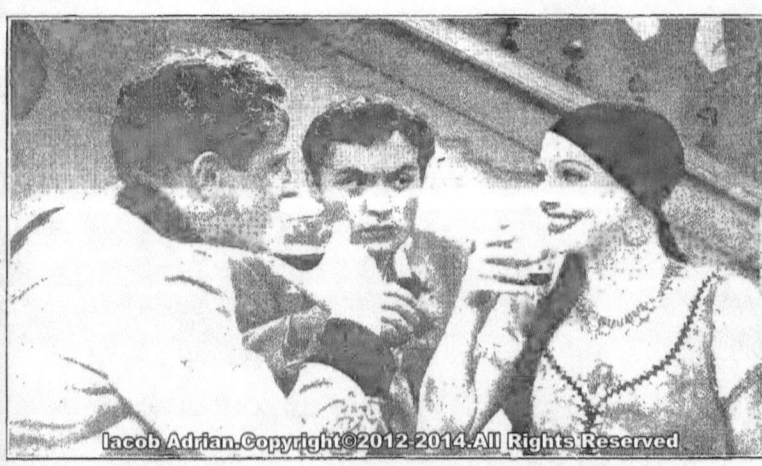

Phillips Holmes, Charles Boyer and Loretta Young as they appear in Fox's forthcoming spectacular production, Caravan

Cross Examining

What do you want to know about the Stars? Use this coupon

THE STARS

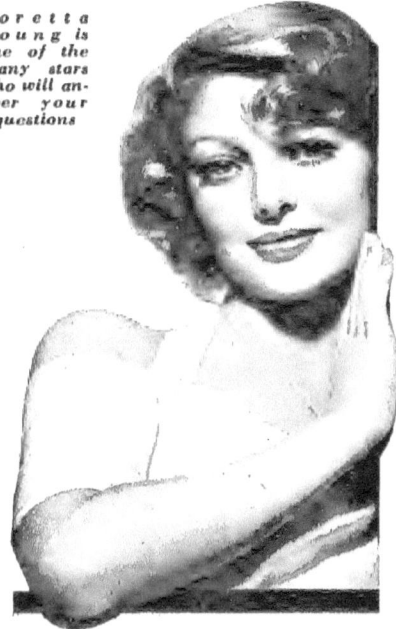

Loretta Young is one of the many stars who will answer your questions

---

The Question Editor,
HOLLYWOOD Magazine,
6605 Hollywood Blvd.,
Hollywood, California.

I should like to ask............................

....

the following question........................

....

....

....

....

....

My name is...

Address ....

It will be impossible to grant personal replies. Questions will be answered only on this page, and those of the most general interest will be given preference.

KATHARINE HEPBURN—Do you ever intend to quit the movies and go back to the stage? I hope so. How tall are you really? According to what I read, you are anywhere from five feet, three inches to five feet, six inches.

I hope to sandwich in an occasional stage play between pictures, but I don't believe I will ever return to the stage permanently. I am really five feet, three inches.

CLARK GABLE—What picture did you enjoy playing in the most?

You've caught me on that question. I've played in so many that I liked that I really don't know which I enjoyed the most. Sorry I can't answer your question a little more definitely.

CECILIA PARKER—What is your address? How old are you? Are you a brunette or a blonde?

You can write to me in care of M-G-M Studio, Culver City, California. I was born April 26, 1905, so I am just twenty-nine years old. I am a blonde.

JEAN HARLOW—What is your address? Would you write to a real good-looking man?

My mailing address is Metro-Goldwyn-Mayer Studio, Culver City, California. I try to answer as much of my fan-mail as possible. Why, yes, I would write to a real good-looking man just as readily as I would write to one not so good-looking.

JACKIE COOPER—How old are you? What color are your eyes? When is your birthday?

I am eleven years old going on twelve. My eyes are blue. I was eleven on September 15.

JOAN BLONDELL—Are you married? What is your real name? How old are you? Have you any children?

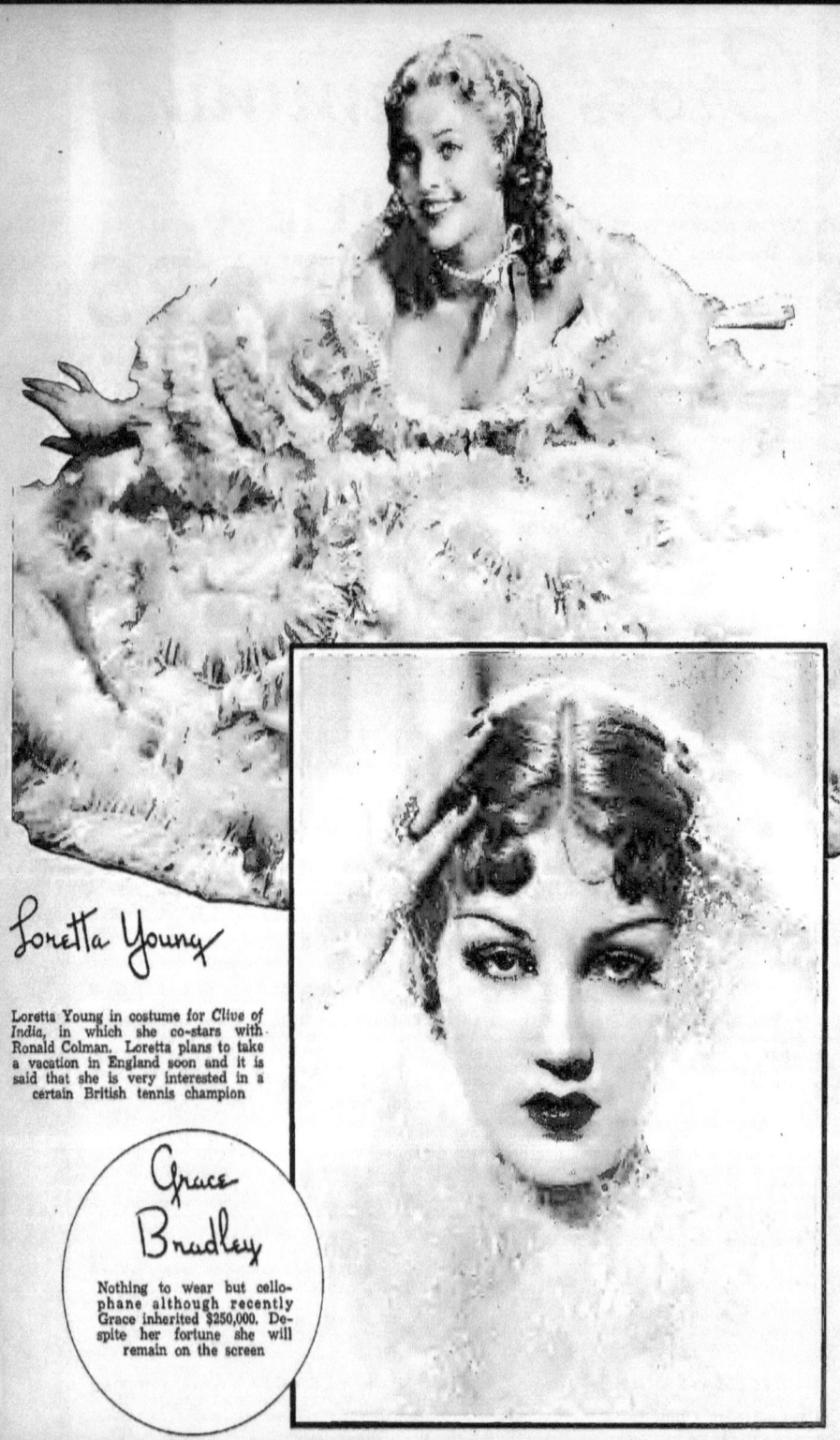

Loretta Young

Loretta Young in costume for *Clive of India*, in which she co-stars with Ronald Colman. Loretta plans to take a vacation in England soon and it is said that she is very interested in a certain British tennis champion

Grace Bradley

Nothing to wear but cellophane although recently Grace inherited $250,000. Despite her fortune she will remain on the screen

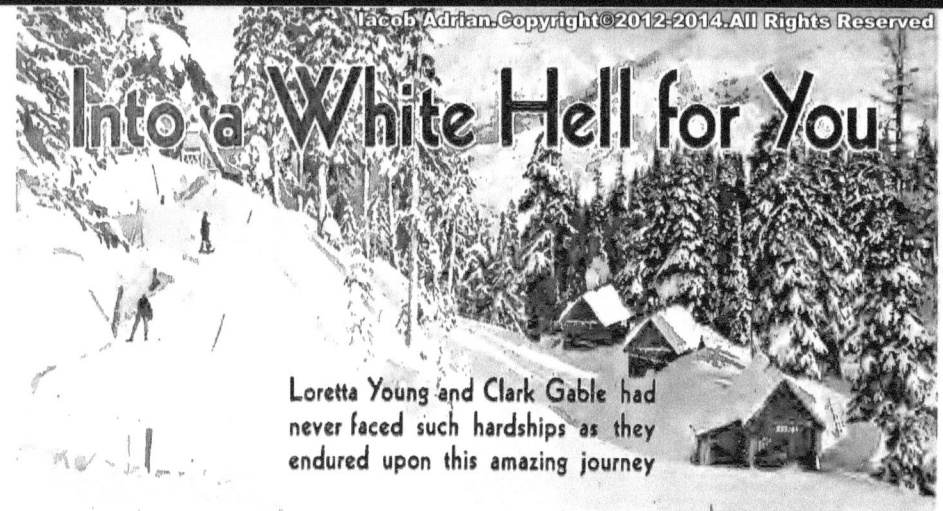

Into a White Hell for You

Loretta Young and Clark Gable had never faced such hardships as they endured upon this amazing journey

by JACK SMALLEY

● As You Movie goers sit back in a comfortable seat in your favorite motion picture theatre, do you ever think of the hardships—sometimes almost incredible hardships—that a group of film workers suffered to make possible your entertainment?

When 20th Century's *Call of the Wild* company left the studio, they planned to be gone ten days or two weeks. But they reckoned without the frigid grasp of a northern winter. Held by the icy blasts of blizzard after blizzard, the weeks lengthened into more than a month of privations from cold and threatened starvation.

Without warning, the blizzards struck, isolating the little group from the base of supplies. Telephone wires were torn down by the storms, and after more than a week, short-wave r a d i o s re-established communications. With food supplies running low, restricted rations were necessary. They did not know, as they carried on, that their hazards were increased by avalanches and washed-out bridges in the floods below their mountainous location. Imprisoned and facing hunger— the photograph above shows how completely they were snowed in —aid finally reached them via relays of snow plows, trucks and dog teams.

● Those Hellish, frozen weeks on location atop snowy Mount Baker in the State of Washington! Difficult to picture, in the midst of California summertime, the incredible hardships suffered by Loretta Young, C l a r k Gable, Jack Oakie, Director William Wellman and others among that intrepid band of the *Call of the Wild* company w h e n snow covered the cabins ten thousand feet above the sea, when open fireplaces failed to heat summer resort hotels with the thermometer twenty below!

"Nobody expects to believe that a pampered film player ever is exposed to real hardships," Loretta told me, "but if you could have seen what we went through—! It was no p r e s s agent's dream, the rigors of that location trip.

"It might not have been so difficult for me had I been accustomed to cold. Although I was born in Salt Lake City, where winter is frigid enough, I was brought to Hollywood when very young, and lived all my life in sunshine and palms. When we got to the jumping off place near Mount Baker, I was unable to adjust myself to the

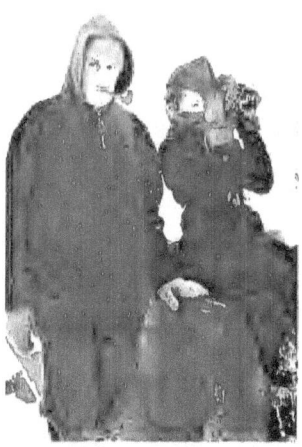

Director William Wellman and his wife, Dorothy Coonan, muffled to the eyes, dared snowslides to reach location

cold. And it was bitterly cold, with worse to come.

"When we attempted to make the location camp on Mount Baker, our party had no sooner been bundled into cars when we met the studio trucks returning. Snowslides had blocked the roads. There was no hotel at the little settlement at Glacier. We were stumped.

● "Fortunately Mr. and Mrs. Graham of Glacier made room for Mr. and Mrs. Reginald Owen, my companion, Mrs. Frances Earle, and me. Bill Wellman and Dorothy, his wife, pushed on by dog sled next morning, and then a snowplow cleared the way for the rest of us. That was our introduction to the hardships to follow.

"A flimsy sound stage had been built near the summer lodge on top of Mount Baker, in case of blizzards. We drew a blizzard immediately, and tried to work on this stage. Wind whistled through it. My nostrils frosted shut, my feet seemed like cakes of ice. In that bitter cold, we could shoot for only a half hour at a time.

"We slept in the cabin annex to the hotel which had burned down, with little heat and all sorts of discomforts, but not a soul complained. Mrs. Clark Gable stuck it out valiantly, but she and I almost lost heart when one night the power plant broke down. Without lights or electric heat, we were ready to freeze to death for dear old 20th Century. I felt so sorry for the crew sent to repair the plant that I forgot my own discomfort, and how we cheered them when they returned, successful, after battling three solid hours to reach the power plant through the snow. One of the boys passed out, and came very close to giving his life to save the rest of us from surely freezing.

"Clark and Jack Oakie and Director Wellman made life bearable with their unfailing good humor—though sometimes Jack also made life almost unbearable with his gags. But you have to forgive him—he is so contrite and innocent looking when he confesses a prank.

● "WE HAD plenty of frozen meat, but we were soon starved for fresh vegetables. I developed a tremendous hankering for a stick of celery—just one little piece of celery would have made me happy. For five days, we couldn't even leave our cramped quarters, with the snow over the tops of windows and a howling blizzard raging. The partitions that divided our chicken-coop rooms were as thin as

and another member of the party crushed a knee cap on the slippery paths, we went around with ski sticks to keep from falling. It was a thrilling experience, but I'd hate to repeat it!"

Their supplies had to be brought in over sixty miles of mountain road from Bellingham, with the constant danger of snow slides blocking the way. All the males in the cast bristled with beards, which collected icicles in that brittle cold weather. Cabin roofs groaned under the weight of 30-foot drifts, windows glowed feebly from what light filtered through the snow.

The power plant episode described by Loretta nearly ended the location

trip. A break occurred in the power line sometime after midnight, and the suffering community knew that all pipe lines would soon freeze and burst. The work of the crew was truly heroic in repairing the damaged line which was found by frantically digging through drifts. No less real was the danger of food shortage when a chinook (warm wind) melted drifts, flooded lower roads, washed out bridges, and no supplies could be brought in. Dog sleds finally got through with provisions in the nick of time.

The picture, all agree, is worth it. *Call of the Wild*, most famous of Jack London's tales, is another triumph for youthful Darryl Zanuck.

Loretta Young, delight of directors and cameramen, is Cecil B. deMille's choice for *The Crusaders*, in which she now finds herself in other difficulties. But the hazards of such a picture will be nothing compared with the incredible hardships she suffered on location in a white hell for you.

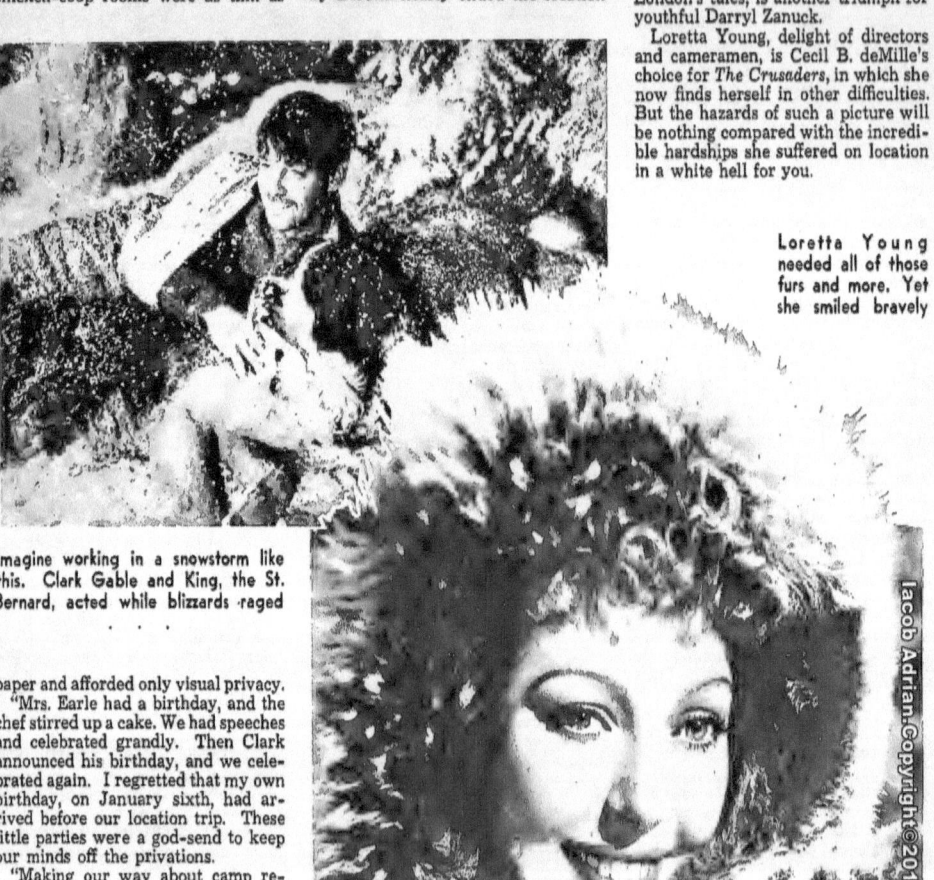

Imagine working in a snowstorm like this. Clark Gable and King, the St. Bernard, acted while blizzards raged . . .

Loretta Young needed all of those furs and more. Yet she smiled bravely

paper and afforded only visual privacy.

"Mrs. Earle had a birthday, and the chef stirred up a cake. We had speeches and celebrated grandly. Then Clark announced his birthday, and we celebrated again. I regretted that my own birthday, on January sixth, had arrived before our location trip. These little parties were a god-send to keep our minds off the privations.

"Making our way about camp required a guide to get us through the maize of deep cut snow paths. They seemed to lead everywhere. One night, we tried to find our way to the mess shack without our guide, Harvey, and became lost. Finally, we saw a light and got back to the cabins, but we were as frightened as we were frozen.

"There was real d a n g e r—avalanches, for one thing—all about us, as we all knew, but the players and crew never became discouraged nor lost heart. Wellman kept things in an uproar. There was never a dull moment if he could help it.

"After Mrs. Earle sprained her ankle

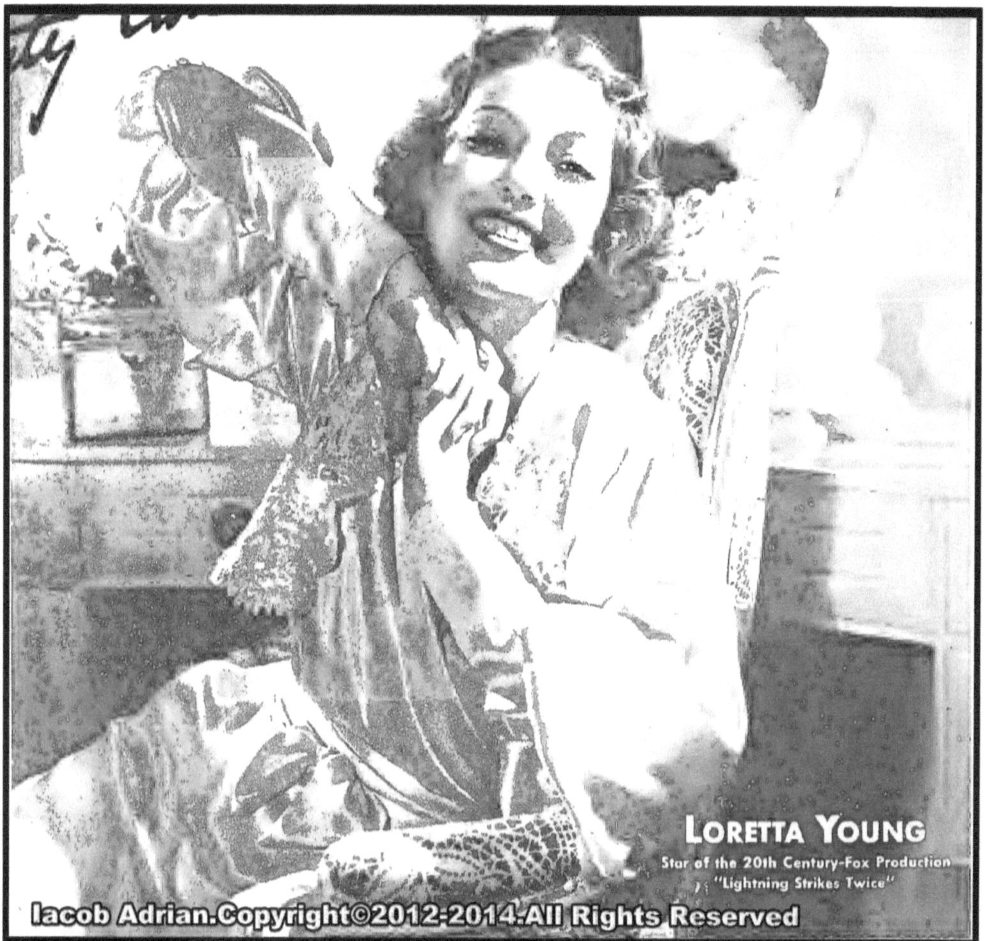

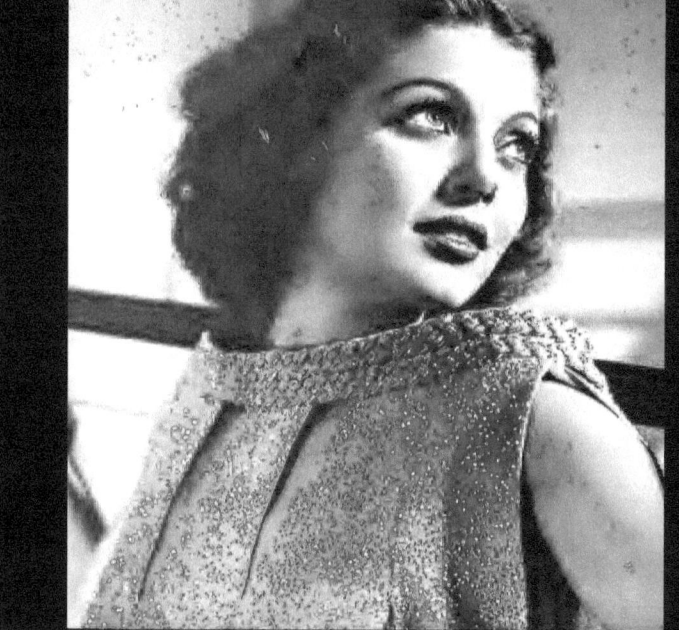

Loretta Young—
Sweet Girl, Smart Dame

THAT HAPPY GLINT, long missing from Loretta Young's eyes, is back again after many stormy months. A year ago she basked warmly in the bright light of popularity. She completed two smash hits, *The Crusades* and *Shanghai*. Every producer was either at her door demanding her services, or lamenting his inability to line her up.

And then it happened, strangely and forebodingly. The radiance faded from

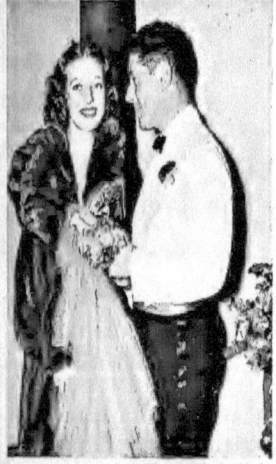

— *Photo by Charles Rhodes*

Has Loretta Young a real romance here? She's being seen frequently with Director Eddie Sutherland at Hollywood affairs. Right, ready for the evening in an exotic gown with a silver fox wrap

her glance, the sparkle from her manner. Serious-faced doctors gathered around, ordered Loretta to take a complete rest before she encountered a complete breakdown.

The ensuing months passed slowly for Loretta. She couldn't help fretting over her enforced vacation, but like a good scout she repaired to the desert and took the rest cure prescribed for her.

Now she is back at work, busy as ever and full of the spontaneous gaiety she has always displayed. She recently finished *The Unguarded Hour* at M-G-M with Franchot Tone and is now doing *Private Number* with Robert Taylor. Knowing that Loretta will soon be on the screen in a thousand home towns over the country, we dug up some interesting material to satisfy fan appetites.

Loretta is not only a sweet girl, she's a smart dame, too. In private life the things she does would make you smile with joy. It's nice to see business acumen alongside lilting personality. And we have a story or two to prove our point. Come with us to the Young household of an evening!

● THE FRONT DOOR BANGED. Mrs. Young and two of her daughters, Sally Blane and Polly Ann Young looked up inquiringly from their books. Rapid footsteps approached the library, petulant footsteps, and then Loretta flung herself into the room.

While she seized a cigarette and flopped into a chair the whole family looked at her in amazement. No word was spoken. No one knew just quite what to say. They'd never seen Loretta in a bad temper. It was something so utterly new that they were flabbergasted. All through dinner she was by turns airy, abstracted and surly, yet there wasn't a word of question or remonstrance spoken. A family with three girls in the profession can recognize a fit of temperament when they see it. . . . But what literally stopped them was the fact that it was Loretta, of all people, who should show signs of the one thing she'd always beefed about in others . . . going Hollywood!

Directly after dinner she went to her room. And it was then that Loretta was stopped cold. Pinned significantly on her door was a large, garish gilt star. There was nothing else, just that. Not a word had been spoken, but that star spoke volumes. Loretta deflated like a balloon. Very slowly and thoughtfully she went into her room to think. A few moments later she could be seen stealing down the back stairs and out into the night.

● THE FRONT DOOR CLOSED with a slight jar.

Mrs. Young and two of her daughters, Sally Blane and Polly Ann Young, looked up from their books. Rapid footsteps approached the library, light, running footsteps, and then Loretta ran in.

"Hello, everybody!" she grinned, "what's new in the world this night? . . . Look! I've got some gimmicks and gadgets here . . ."

Walking around the room as she spoke, she plopped a package into the laps of each of her sisters and her mother, some hankies for Sally, hose for Polly Ann and perfume for her mother. Peace offerings? Not exactly; more in the nature of small, graceful apologies for her previous stormy entrance.

The conversation was gay and animated for the rest of the evening and entirely without a single reference to the uncomfortable interlude. They ended up by playing bridge and having the usual swell time they have when all four are home together. Parenthetically, let us add, that that was the one and only burst of temperament ever actually recorded against Loretta.

She may be an important luminary in Hollywood skies today, but at home she is no more important than any of the rest of the family, no more important than she was eight years ago when she was just an

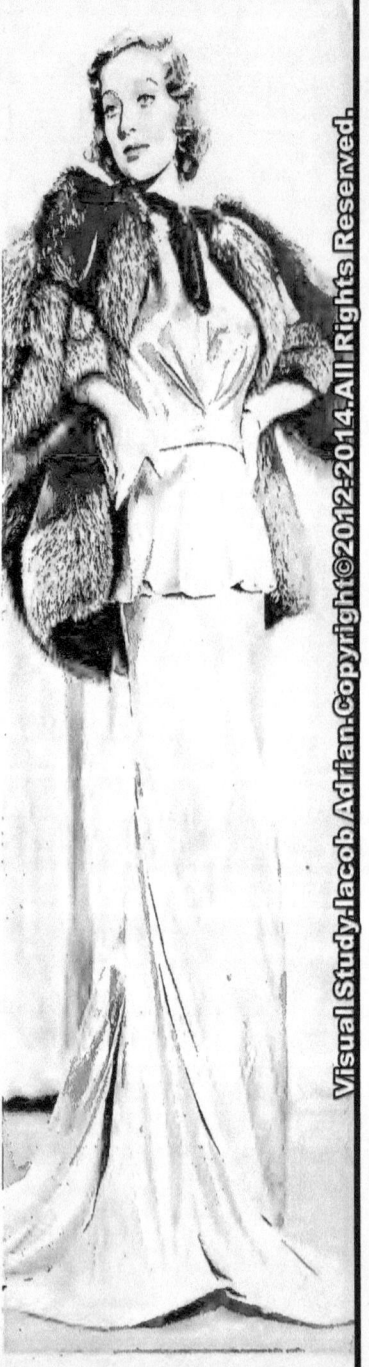

Loretta Young— Sweet Girl, Smart Dame

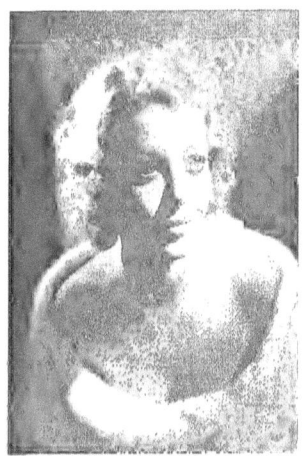

Loretta Young is back in pictures after a long rest prescribed by her doctors. You'll find her more beautiful than ever

attractive kid who hadn't filled out into womanhood yet and used to tag around the sets after her then brilliantly scintillating sister, Sally Blane.

● FEW OF US WHO SAW Loretta inconspicuously about town in those days ever would have thought that that kid would some day be the absolute tops, big enough to have none other than the Great C. B. De Mille hold up production on one of his super-epics, *The Crusades*, because she was snowed in up in the mountains.

But don't think that Loretta attained that prominence by being all sweetness and light. She is, in reality, two separate and distinct people at home and at the studio. She's lived in this business all her life and knows it as only she could. She's learned a lot on the way up. Particularly she has discovered that allowing oneself to be imposed upon is a fool's game in any business, but most especially in pictures.

Let us make that plain. When Loretta first went into pictures on a long term contract she was just seventeen. Her contract had to be approved by the courts and it was stipulated that, being a minor, she could not work more than eight hours a day. The State appointed a lady to look after her in the studio and on the sets to see to it that the laws on child labor were upheld. But all that was extremely irksome to an energetic and ambitious young girl. She wanted to work till she dropped —anything to speed her success.

And that is just what she did do— worked till she dropped. For over two years, one picture after another, she would leave the set with the guardian, start to take her make-up off and then stall around until the lady had left. Instantly Loretta donned the war-paint again and was back on the set till two and three in the morning. She kept it up till the family had to send her to the hospital with a nervous break-down.

But even then Loretta was undaunted. It was not until an official from the studio came to her in the hospital with the word that she was to start another picture in two days that she began to see the light. It was either work or the studio would magnanimously grant her a vacation without pay until she could . . . It is typical of Loretta that she has always felt sorry for the poor duck who had to deliver the news to her. He hated the job, but just had to obey orders.

Of course, conditions like that are all changed now, but in those few moments in the hospital bed little Miss Young who would work like a fool for the spirit of the thing became another person. She got smart, smart the hard way!

From that day to this she has never worked five minutes beyond the eight hours that are specified in her contract. Why should she? Advantage had been taken of her in no uncertain way and she decided that that was a sucker's game. You mustn't get the idea that she's tough about things. She's not. I know of no one any more popular with crews and casts than she. Even when she's standing on her rights she does it in such a sweet and evenly-disposed manner that no one could take exception to it—and she never takes any stand unless she's right!

A strange little quirk in her make-up about the hours she works is shown in her complete willingness to take stills and home-sittings for hours on end. Most players abhor that task. Try it yourself sometime—sitting for three or four hundred differently posed pictures with a dozen changes of costume and being forced to make each one register with a definite and lively expression. It is far more exhausting and monotonous work than acting, but Loretta will work until the cameramen drop in her own home. She's not afraid of work, not afraid of any task that comes along in daily life—but she won't be imposed upon.

● AT HOME IF THE MAID is busy when Loretta gets up she'd as soon go out in the kitchen and perk her own breakfast coffee. Her mother certainly would —and the two sisters—so, as she figures it, why not herself?

Loretta is such a completely normal, average every-day human being that she's well-nigh impossible to clearly portray. Theirs is the average, normally well-off American family in New York or Massilion, Ohio. None of this oft-repeated talk of Hollywood extravagances and luxuries beyond reason and income.

And yet, at the same time, Loretta is the girl who has learned every rope in Hollywood on her way up. Frequently studios make a practice of giving cast and crew substantial proportionate bonuses when a picture has been brought in under schedule and is obviously a success. Just recently Loretta was offered a bonus amounting to $10,000 . . . and she turned it down! Very sweetly did she thank them and when they pressed it on her she said, "No, but if you really want me to have a bonus you can give me a trip to New York, all expenses paid, and a new car."

She outsmarted them, and they knew it and admired her for it. Had she accepted the cash bonus she would have had to pay an income tax on it which the studio would have been exempted of, but on the basis of a car and a trip for the bonus it was the studio and not Loretta who paid the additional Government tax. . . . And that is what is known out here as figuring all the angles. That is plenty smart!

—WILLIAM ULMAN, JR.

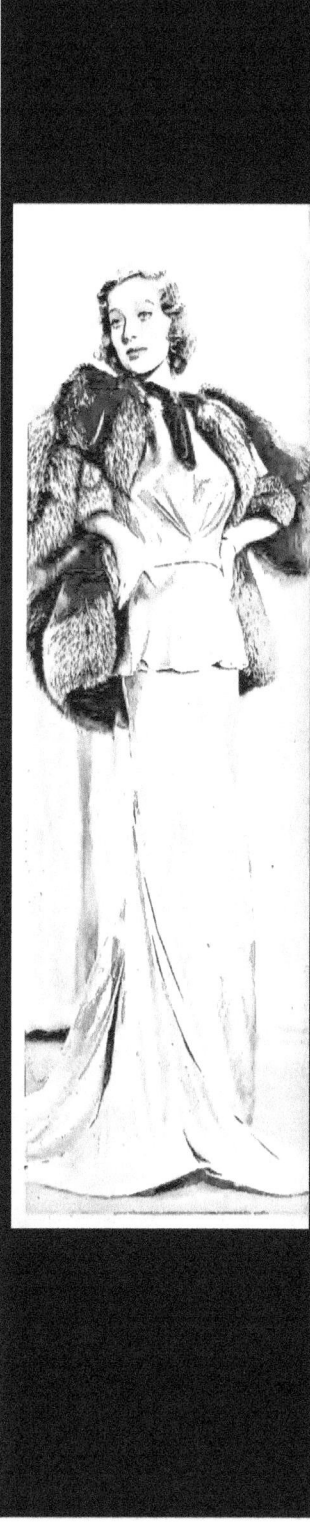

They Couldn't Say No to Loretta

Loretta Young, just finished with one epic, is rushing into another. This time 20th Century-Fox is starring her along with Janet Gaynor and Constance Bennett in *Ladies in Love*. It is ticklish business, putting three stars with equal billing in one picture, in addition to featuring Simone Simon. The studio will tell you all must get an even break, have equally good dressing rooms, and be treated entirely on a par. A big job.

Loretta Young's *Ramona* is a materialization of the incredible, doggedly engineered by that firm and forthright young woman herself.

From the hour she heard that 20th Century-Fox intended making *Ramona*, Miss Young set out after the rôle, because:

She is at bottom an incorrigible mystic, and believed deeply in her gift for bringing to its religious flights a special emotional integrity.

She naturally wanted one of the year's plums.

She sensed that a lot of people—which indeed they did—would be amused at the idea of fair Loretta Young impersonating an Indian maid; and Loretta Young has a special fondness for converting the scoffer.

It is no secret that she had to sell everyone at the studio, from the "little white English cottage" down. Which she did. Quite as much in exhaustion as in compliance, Messrs. Zanuk, Wurtzel, et al finally agreed to a test.

If Miss Young went into the test with full confidence in her incorruptible face, she emerged with Technicolors flying. It was a fact: in beige make-up and black wig she was a Ramona that put a stop to the Oberon-Colbert talk. She could do it.

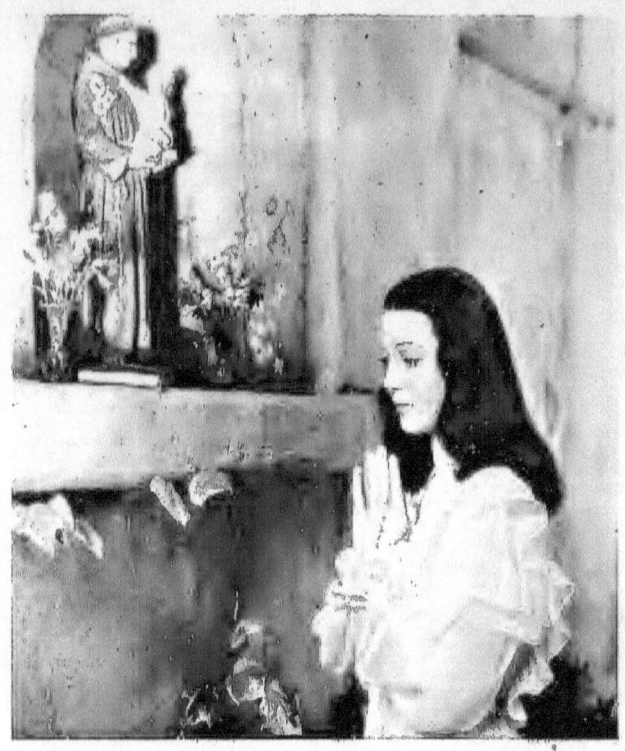

Loretta becomes *Ramona* in the famous American classic now being filmed in Technicolor by 20th Century-Fox. Loretta got the rôle by refusing to take no for an answer

She Faced the Music

● If Loretta Young is a frail mechanism, she is an efficient one, fired by as sharp and galling ambition as ever possessed a little-girl-bound-to-get-the-best-of-things. She fought for the rôle when she should have been in bed, and she played it out—the whole bitter seven weeks of it in the raw wind and blazing

[Continued on page 62]

"HANDIES" & Doggies » » » » » LOUISE LATIMER & "SQUEEZIT"

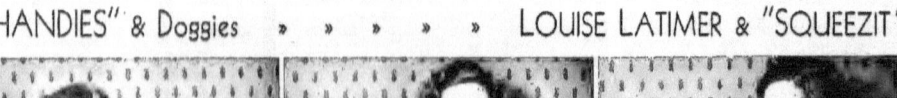

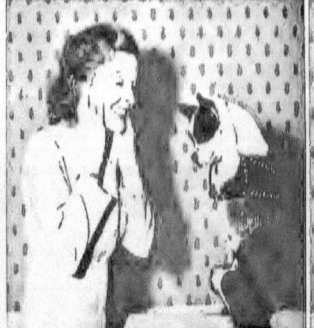

You saw them in *Bunker Bean*, and aren't they clever! Here Louise and the pup "see no evil," portraying it by using

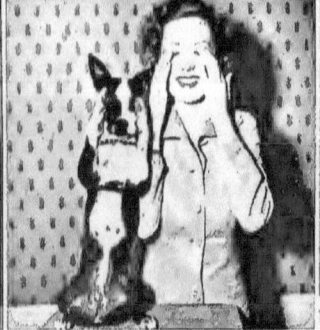

"handies," or "pawsies" from the dog's point of view. It's all in a spirit of fun, and "Squeezit" likes to do the "hear no evil"

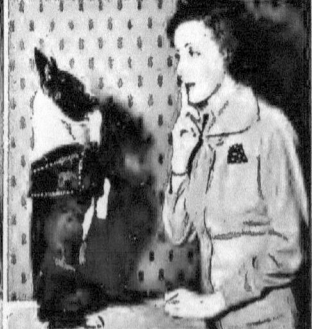

routine. Now they finish this exclusive act for HOLLYWOOD Magazine with an account of the last of the trinity—"speak no evil!"

They Couldn't Say No to Loretta

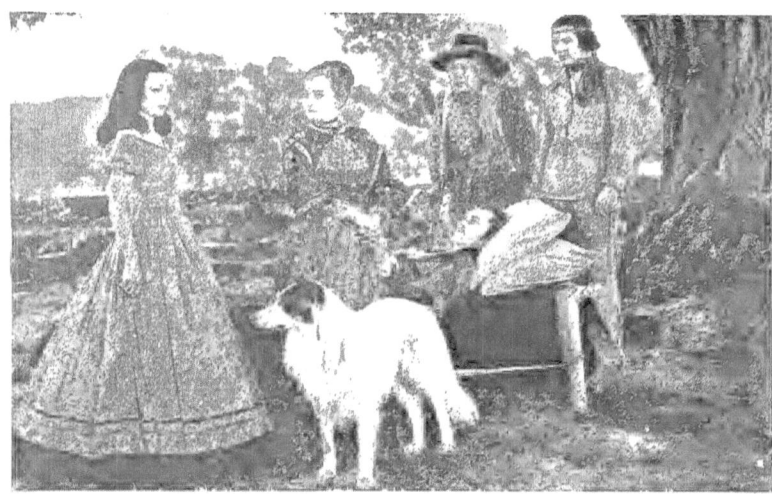

Ramona has a varied and delightful cast. Among those you will see are these above: Loretta Young, Pauline Frederick, Kent Taylor, J. Carrol Naish, and Don Ameche

sun—when she should have been lazing around the shore.

Withal, she was on the set at seven, and she was still there at five. Most of the time she was dog-tired, but she always rose and flung herself into the scene, even if the location doctor had to stand by between times with a dropper full of adrenalin for her tired, blood-shot eyes. She spared no one—including herself—if she saw any excuse for a re-take.

A gregarious person, she resigned herself to seven weeks of nothing but work and sleep. At five o'clock she left the set for her cottage, had a massage and shower, ate a light meal and fell into bed.

The frequent trips from the location to town and back again were not exactly restful. It was 135 miles and more from Hollywood to Warner Hot Springs, nearest village to the *Ramona* set.

The ultimate destination of Warners Hot Springs is in the foothills. Mountains are near, and hot deserts, too. It is a remarkable country, typical of the setting represented in the famous classic.

The capricious mountain weather veered between bitter cold and blazing hot. She caught cold, and she wilted from heat. Her skin chapped and it blistered. And she drove herself along, for she had promised herself she would materialize the incredible.

Ramona should do well. The steadily-improving color camera makes the most of the rarely beautiful terrain—great sweeps of mountain meadows, with towering old cottonwoods and green willows, mountain streams and lakes and "chases" shot from two miles straight above, sweeping over forty miles of plateau.

Raised in a Convent

⊙ AND SO LORETTA YOUNG, who entered moving pictures through a piece of precocious guile, lifts her dainty feet over another hurdle.

It was some 20 years ago that widowed Mother Young brought her starry-eyed moppets from the arid reaches of Utah to the New Bagdad.

After a childhood spent mostly in convents (Loretta developed the *Ramona* fixation in Ramona convent, Alhambra, when she could hardly read), the Young girls—Polly Ann, Loretta and Sally (Blane) began dropping by studios, and the big-eyed trio soon became a familiar sight around casting offices.

One day Mervyn LeRoy telephoned the populous Young home to invite Polly Ann by for an interview. Polly Ann was away at a Girl Scout camp, but Loretta, who even then knew Opportunity from the grocer's boy, borrowed one of Polly Ann's dresses and caught the street car. The gateman, who has stopped many older heads, had no defense against her *entre*: "I'm Miss Young. Mr. LeRoy expects me."

Clad in the armor of half-truth, she sailed through to LeRoy's office, and the first important man who ever tried to say no to little Loretta Young found out that in the end it was easier to say yes.

Once only—and early—did she stray from her single-minded pursuit of gilded glory. At seventeen, she married Grant Withers. It was soon over, and she has since devoted her energies, with few interruptions, to the furtherment of her drive upon the stony battlements of Hollywood.

She draws a deep satisfaction from the adoring company of Edward Sutherland, the producer, but few expect that she will marry him. He is a veteran of the divorce courts, an affront to her Catholicism, and there seems no room in the tight little Young cosmos for any new people.

She made an eloquent speech—unconsciously—a few weeks before she began *Ramona*.

"You know," she told someone sweetly, "the people at the studio were lovely to me when I was sick. Orchids? Great baskets of them. And candy, and lovely jellied soups from the Vendome. No one could have been more considerate.

"But they stopped my paycheck."

love IS news...

...when this romantic trio
make their new kind of love!

Sweethearts who might as well live in glass houses...their kisses crash the headlines and their nights of romance sell "Extras" in the morning! When they thrill ...the world thrills with them... and so will you!—especially over Tyrone Power, the new star sensation of "Lloyds of London" in a role even more sensational!

TYRONE   LORETTA   DON
POWER · YOUNG · AMECHE
in
"LOVE IS NEWS"
with

SLIM SUMMERVILLE · DUDLEY DIGGES
WALTER CATLETT · GEORGE SANDERS
JANE DARWELL · STEPIN FETCHIT
PAULINE MOORE

Directed by Tay Garnett
Associate Producers Earl Carroll and Harold Wilson
DARRYL F. ZANUCK In Charge of Production

20th CENTURY FOX

Hollywood Charm School

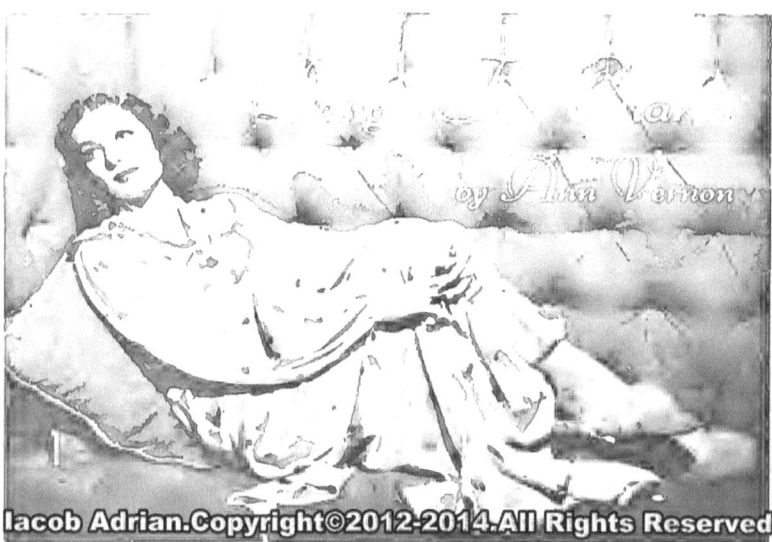

Beautiful Loretta Young reveals the secrets of feminine fascination

"A CHARMING GIRL"—those are words which never fail to challenge the interest of men and the attention of women.

I had heard the compliment applied so often to Loretta Young that wild horses couldn't have kept me from accepting an invitation to visit her on the set of *Cafe Metropole* at the 20th Century-Fox studio. I was going to find out, first hand, about all this vaunted charm!

When I arrived, Loretta was rehearsing a street scene with Tyrone Power, Jr., strolling slowly up and down a stretch of pavement as a camera crane moved ahead to pick up the action. It was pretty obvious that this was work combined with pleasure. I couldn't believe that all those smiles were for art's sake alone!

Even at a distance, Loretta's eyes appeared amazingly large and blue against her brown screen make-up. Her costume was a dream of chic. Full-length cape, dress and hat, all made of soft tan suede, with two floating panels of brown chiffon extending from her hat to the bottom of her cape in back.

How much of charm, I wondered, could in every case be attributed to beauty of face, figure and costuming? Loretta herself supplied the answer as we chatted between scenes a few minutes later.

"It is difficult to define charm," she said, "and yet it is certainly a girl's greatest asset. I should say that charm was a combination of physical attractiveness and personality. No matter what her ambitions in life, a girl must first impress someone with her appearance and then with her personality and that someone is usually a man.

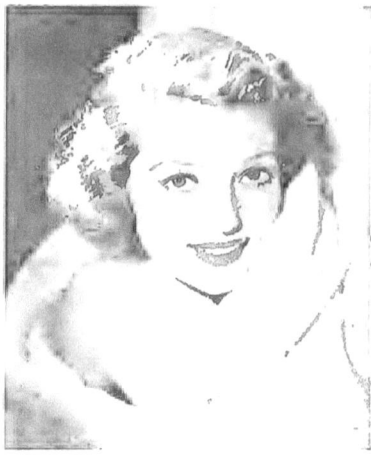

Loretta believes in that well-scrubbed look as an adjunct of feminine charm

"An unattractive first impression may ruin her chances of getting any farther."

If physical attractiveness was a good half of charm, then what was to be the salvation of homely girls, I asked.

"Physical attractiveness," Loretta said, "does not mean beauty in the sense of perfect features or perfect figure. But, to me, it does mean complete *femininity* in appearance, dress and manner. The more feminine a girl is, the more likely she is to be attractive to men.

"The foremost characteristic of femininity is daintiness. Spotless clothing, soft clean hair, a clear skin, carefully manicured nails, fragrance of perfume—those are the things which suggest femininity and they are the things which

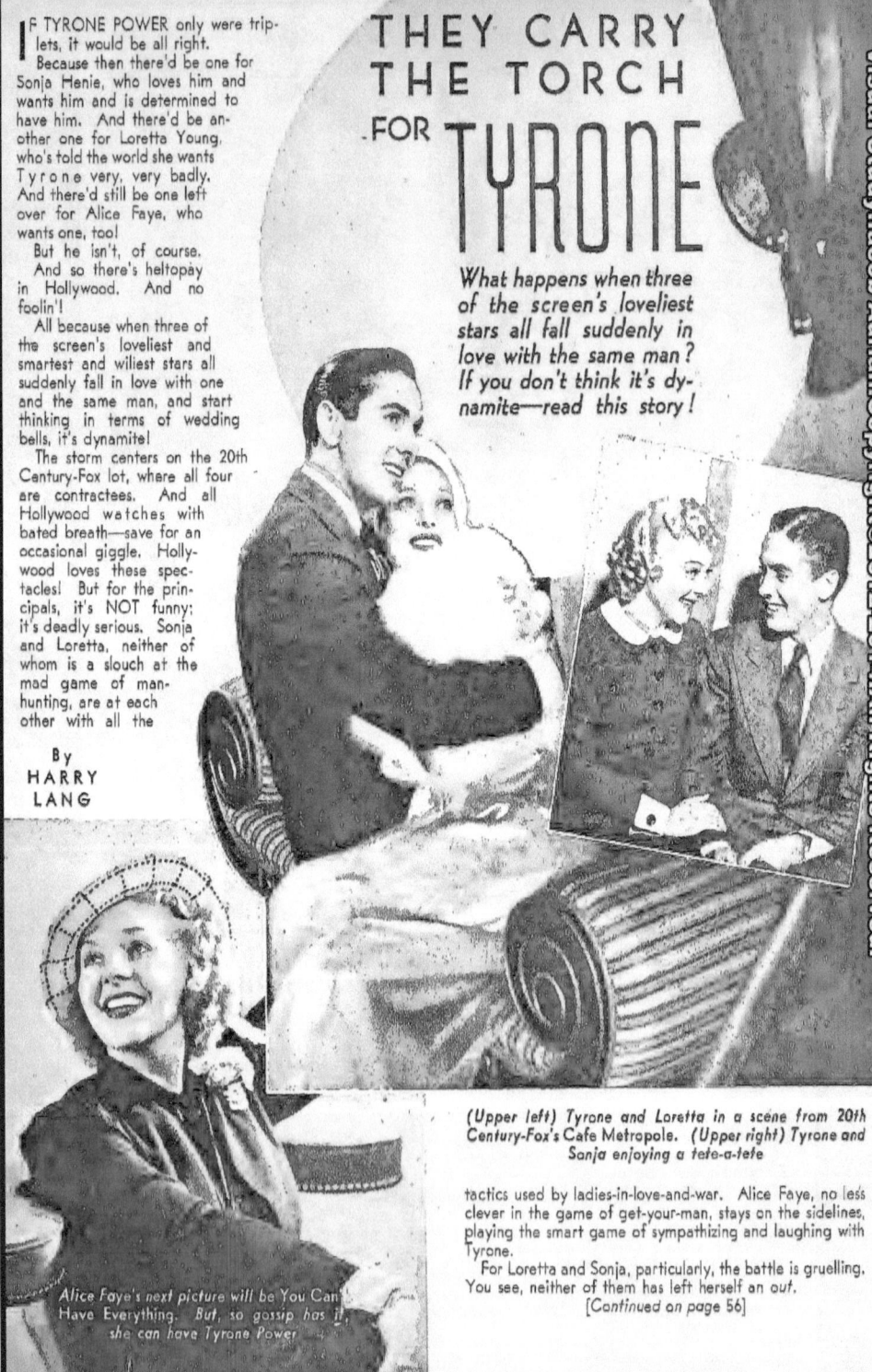

THEY CARRY THE TORCH FOR

TYRONE

IF TYRONE POWER only were triplets, it would be all right.

Because then there'd be one for Sonja Henie, who loves him and wants him and is determined to have him. And there'd be another one for Loretta Young, who's told the world she wants Tyrone very, very badly. And there'd still be one left over for Alice Faye, who wants one, too!

But he isn't, of course.

And so there's heltopay in Hollywood. And no foolin'!

All because when three of the screen's loveliest and smartest and wiliest stars all suddenly fall in love with one and the same man, and start thinking in terms of wedding bells, it's dynamite!

The storm centers on the 20th Century-Fox lot, where all four are contractees. And all Hollywood watches with bated breath—save for an occasional giggle. Hollywood loves these spectacles! But for the principals, it's NOT funny; it's deadly serious. Sonja and Loretta, neither of whom is a slouch at the mad game of man-hunting, are at each other with all the

By
HARRY
LANG

What happens when three of the screen's loveliest stars all fall suddenly in love with the same man? If you don't think it's dynamite—read this story!

(Upper left) Tyrone and Loretta in a scene from 20th Century-Fox's Cafe Metropole. (Upper right) Tyrone and Sonja enjoying a tete-a-tete

tactics used by ladies-in-love-and-war. Alice Faye, no less clever in the game of get-your-man, stays on the sidelines, playing the smart game of sympathizing and laughing with Tyrone.

For Loretta and Sonja, particularly, the battle is gruelling. You see, neither of them has left herself an out.

[Continued on page 56]

Alice Faye's next picture will be You Can't Have Everything. But, so gossip has it, she can have Tyrone Power

IDOLS PAY

FOR THEIR PEDESTALS

Screen stars have a fine time . . . some of the time
but the greater the fame, the higher the price paid
and Loretta Young tells you just how it happens

By SERENA BRADFORD

"Do you realize," said Loretta Young as they called her to go on the set, "that acting before a camera is only one-quarter of the job of being a star? And do you realize what a player has to give up—the ordinary privileges and comforts other people enjoy—in order to gain star rating?"

With this, in an extraordinary and very handsome pair of hostess pajamas ending in a long train that swished, she swept to that spot beneath the hot, white lights where a scene of *Second Honeymoon* was in progress. She left me at the doorway of the trailer-dressing-room to digest her words, to figure out the other three-quarters of the star job as well as the strange sacrifices at which she hinted. Loretta had spoken seriously. She was in dead earnest.

Yet to see the lady, gay and lovely, joking with other players before the sequence began, nobody would suppose she had a care in the world. Surely, being a star is one of the nicest jobs imaginable. Beautiful face, beautiful figure—and hovering beauty experts at hand to keep them so. Beautiful clothes, and the right people to design them. Beautiful income. Not to mention beautiful waves of idolization and envy from every sector of the globe. The darling of unnumbered million fans. . . .

"Yes, it's inspiring, it's splendid," Loretta acknowledged when she returned to the dressing-room, "I'm thankful for it, and it makes me glad. But, on the other hand, what does all this involve in sheer surrender of the things a human being most desires?

"Do you realize that to be a star, a girl frequently has to forego the things dearest to any woman's heart? Not love, but the privileges of privacy when that love comes along? Not decency and high standards, but (only too often!) personal reputation, unfairly clouded, no matter how straight and decent she may in reality be?

"I'm well aware of the gratitude a star owes for the fact that she *is* a star. But I'm also aware

of the malice that stardom seems to bring out as candy brings out ants. A conspicuous position seems to attract this malice whether the victim's a star or a statesman.

"Idols pay for their pedestals! They pay in cruel and unjustified whisperings circulated about them; they pay for public prestige with their private peace of mind, no matter how crazy and unfounded the gossip may be. In politics or pictures, and especially in pictures, the moment a man or woman achieves a pedestal the whispering campaign begins. I don't know why. Perhaps psychologists do. Not for the majority of people, because most people are good and wholesome, but for the cynical, the comparatively few, a star is a target. And unfortunately the cynics have the loudest voices."

She flung out shapely fingers in a philosophic gesture. No bitterness darkened her shining eyes; she has too much sense to grow bitter about an annoyance that befalls each and sundry when Fame arrives, for Fame never arrives without Gossip tagging at heel.

But while no bitterness gleamed in Loretta's look, there gleamed no resignation, either. What gleamed was the determination for once to speak her mind on the subject. Calmly, but completely.

"My little sister came home crying not long ago," she said. Then she paused and again flung out her fingers, this time in a motion indicating many varied threads caught up into one handful.

"It's all mixed to-gether," she explained, "that part of the star job which doesn't involve acting before a camera, and that phase of it which involves"—her voice supplied quotation marks—"what 'they say.' One's bound up with the other.

"Well, my little sister came home crying. She ran to her room and threw herself on the bed and cried as if her heart would break. 'Darling, what *is* it?' I asked. 'Oh, do you know what the girls at school said

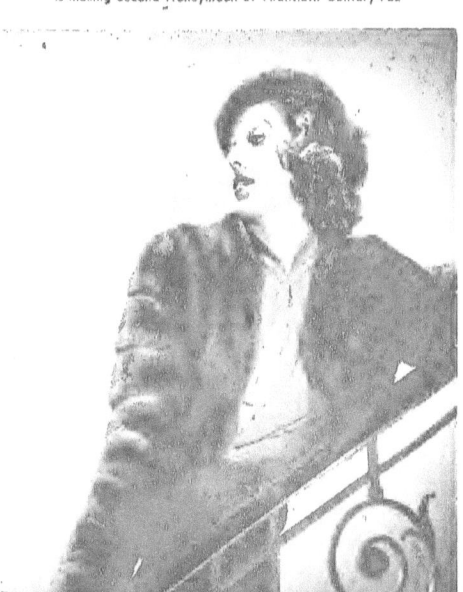

Lovely Loretta is ready for winter's harshest winds in a mink bolero, blouse of soft suede and a cap that is faintly reminiscent of Daniel Boone's famous headgear. She is now to be seen in *Wife, Doctor and Nurse*, and is making *Second Honeymoon* at Twentieth Century-Fox

Tyrone Knows an Answer

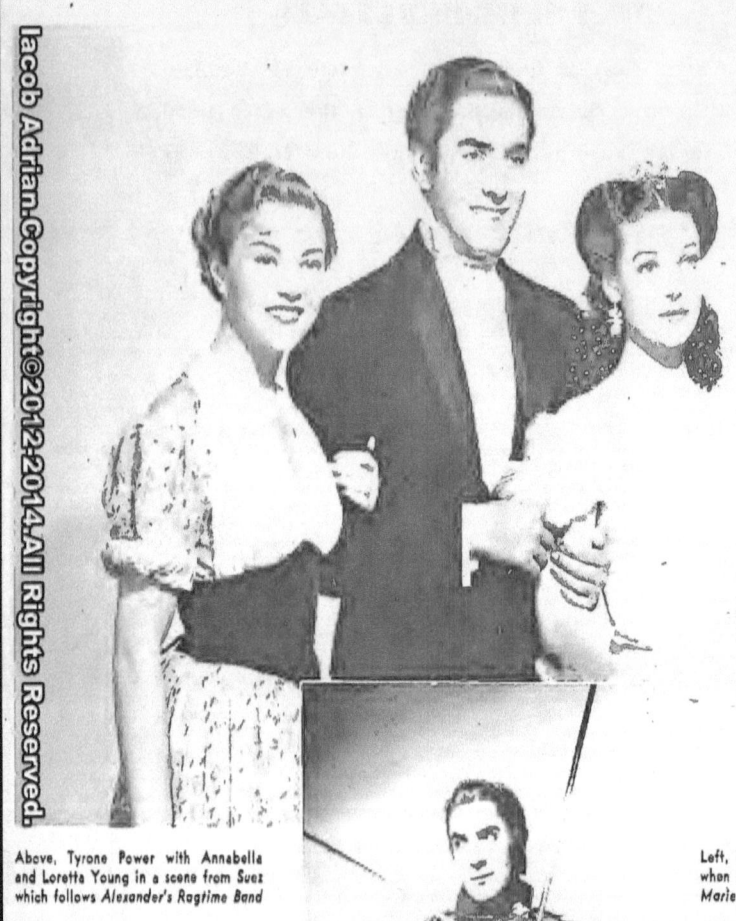

Above, Tyrone Power with Annabella and Loretta Young in a scene from *Suez* which follows *Alexander's Ragtime Band*

Left, Power can put up a good fight, when necessary, as he demonstrates in *Marie Antoinette*, to s t r i k i n g effect

Young Mr. Power has a hot temper but he also has a quick wit and he has learned that one is much more useful than the other in any career

By SONIA LEE

■ It was undoubtedly the incident of the sour-pickle crock which first impressed upon Tyrone Power the saving grace of meeting situations which promised to be embarrassing armed with a sense of humor.

He must have been all of seven when he was discovered mapping out a first-class tummyache by stuffing himself with the crunchy, dark-green, tempting but forbidden delicacy.

There was practically no pause between his mother's demand for an explanation and his glib reply.

"Teacher," he explained seriously, "called me sweet. It's sissy for boys to be sweet. So I'm eating pickles."

There was no answer to that alibi. Ever since then, Tyrone has been turning away wrath, extricating himself from delicate situations, getting at least a laugh a day by that quick wit and subtle sense of humor.

"It's a bit earlyish for philosophy," Tyrone observed, taking measure of the eleven o'clock sun, "but life is a roller-coaster, and the job is to keep your hat on your head when you make the dizzy drops and take the steep curves. You can't do it unless you get a lot of fun as you go along."

■ As a test of a man's innate sense of humor, nothing better has ever been devised than desert sequences. In *Suez*, Tyrone's latest production, much of the action is concerned with the building of the canal, uniting the Red Sea and the Mediterranean. Twentieth Century-Fox carted something like twelve hundred

Tyrone Knows an Answer

carloads of sand from the Santa Monica Beach to the studio, and created a tidy little desert of its own, complete even to the oasis and dim blue mountains in the distance.

For weeks everyone in the *Suez* company ate and breathed sand. When the wind machines were set in action for the typhoon scenes, everyone took on that misty pallor which a nice coating of sand gives.

Tyrone spent an hour after his daily stint was done, digging sand out of his hair, his eyes, his nostrils and his ears.

You would think that under those conditions Tyrone's ability to get fun out of any situation would temporarily go into moth-balls. On the contrary it seemed to thrive. Perhaps, because it challenged his funny-bone.

■ The matter of the donkey was definitely a challenge. Now the animal-actor was used in the scene where Tyrone meets Annabella, who plays the part of Toni, the impish girl who loves Ferdinand de Lesseps, (Tyrone Power), the builder of the *Suez*.

The donkey hired was of a tractable and gentle temperament. It obeyed its trainer's commands perfectly. It made friends with every person on the set.

With everyone except Tyrone. No matter how many juicy apples and succulent carrots he offered, no matter the pleading tones in his voice, the donkey would look at him arrogantly, swish its ears, and trot off disdainfully. The company made clucking noises of sympathy at Tyrone's bewilderment.

Tyrone didn't see the trainer making signs behind his back. But he knew that all wasn't on the up-and-up. No one suspected that his deepening gloom was the fore-runner of planned mischief.

That evening Tyrone made an excursion to Daisy's stall. With him was a man who had been training animals for the movies for years. He was leading Bessie, who might have been Daisy's twin sister.

Daisy was gently led away. Bessie took her place— a tutored Bessie, who in an hour of intensive study learned to take commands only from Tyrone, to follow him at a movement of the hand, to nudge him affectionately.

The following morning, the scenes of the day before which included the donkey, were continued. But with what a difference! No one could do a thing with that blamed donkey. In addition, Daisy's trainer had been called away by a seemingly urgent message, and he had been told not to hurry back because no trouble with Daisy was anticipated.

And here were scenes to be done. The sun was hot and getting hotter. The sand was scorching. And tempers were getting short. Who would have thought that nice, amiable and obliging donkey would hold up production?

"Suppose you let me see what I can do?" Tyrone suggested mildly.

"You?" everyone chorused. "That donkey won't have anything to do with you.

Or did you forget about yesterday?"

But condescendingly, Tyrone was permitted to try anyway.

And wonder of wonders! That donkey did everything but turn somersaults when Tyrone spoke to her. The scenes went through without a hitch. In fact, at amazing speed!

No one could figure it out! There was mystery in this! For a week the puzzle of the donkey haunted those who had tried to fix up Tyrone. They were losing sleep over it. And finally they asked Tyrone for the answer.

"So you want to know, do you?" Tyrone asked. "Well, Daisy wasn't Daisy. She was Bessie!"

Tyrone hadn't had so much fun in a week of Sundays as he did watching the crestfallen faces of the conspirators. Definitely, but definitely, the joke was on them.

■ Even the law has come off second-best in a bout with Tyrone's wit.

When he was serving his acting apprenticeship in New York, he shared a walkup apartment with a friend. Both boys were a bit on the loud side when they came in from their theatre chores at one or two o'clock in the morning.

The tenant below them had no appreciation for the artistic temperament. And he would howl loud and long over their disturbance of his sleep.

His special manner of retaliation was to stick a wad of gum against their bell at five o'clock in the morning, the hour he went to work. The bell would continue sounding its alarm until one of the disgusted boys would come down to pry out the gum.

It went on for days—this noisy feud. And so the boys thought it might be a good idea to give the gentleman a taste of his own medicine. Every night when they came in, they rang their neighbor's bell persistently. The clatter would have waked the dead.

One night the shopkeeper was in a special fury. He'd fix 'em. He'd fix those two good-for-nothings. Actors, humph! He called the police. And a couple of uniforms suddenly materialized at Tyrone's side, while he was taking his turn at bell-ringing.

"Want somebody?" they asked.

"Yes, yes indeed," Tyrone came back quick as a flash. "There's an early rehearsal and I am trying to wake up Tyrone Power. That guy sleeps like a log."

The officers were perplexed. "We got a complaint somebody was creating a disturbance. But you gotta a right to ring the doorbell of somebody you know. Let's go up and pound on your friend's door." Cops could be very suspicious characters.

Up went Tyrone flanked by the law. For an instant he lagged behind as the door opened. Just long enough to signal his buddy to keep quiet.

"Oh, there you are, Mr. Power," Tyrone didn't give anybody a chance to say a word. "Say, you certainly sleep hard.

"I've been ringing your bell for twenty minutes. Rehearsal tomorrow, early. We've been trying to get word to you for hours."

The officers scratched their heads in perplexity. They were murmuring—"People are crazy," as they clattered down the stairs.

"Whew, that was a close one," Tyrone sighed in relief. Jail just wasn't on his program.

Their neighbor moved from there!

■ The most amusing story Tyrone tells points his special and distinct sense of humor.

He was appearing in the New York production of *Romeo and Juliet*, and for the purposes of his part, he had to wear his hair long. "Almost a Garbo bob, it was!" Even today he recalls that embarrassing haircut with resentment.

"It was late December but the Christmas Spirit had passed me up. I wasn't going to expose myself to the stares of shoppers. As it was, I was skulking between the theatre and my room, taking the alleys to do it. I did shove my hair under my hat, but I looked sort of peculiar with my hat perched precariously on the very top of my head.

"But the last day before Christmas, I decided people would be too busy to look at me closely, even with my hat sticking on so queerly. So I went shopping, with my hair carefully tucked up under my biggest, tightest hat.

"All was well. No one had given me a second glance. I was returning home with parcels dangling by their strings from every one of my fingers. And a long roll of Christmas tissue under my arm.

"I had fished out a nickel to pay my bus fare before getting on, but in the rush for the doors my coin slipped and dropped to the floor. The conductor wasn't obliging. He wouldn't pick it up. So somehow, I scrooched down to the floor, and by luck retrieved it. But my hat had remained in the air, resting peacefully on the shoulders of two passengers.

"I stood up, wormed into my hat. But my hair had dropped down. Instead of a passable-looking boy, I suddenly emerged under the gaze of the horrified passengers, as some strange creature with dangling locks.

"The bus swayed and I hit with a thud a passenger's midriff. I turned around to apologize and the roll of tissue swatted the gentleman behind me smack in the face. I was becoming a menace. Everyone was glowering and growling at me. But we were packed so tight that for ten blocks, I am certain, my feet didn't even touch the floor, and no one could move away from my immediate and dangerous vicinity. My Christmas Spirit was rapidly oozing out.

"When my stop came, everybody was eager to pull the bell for me. I was a good riddance—this person who looked like a fugitive from a psychopathic ward."

But Tyrone's troubles weren't over. The driver was in a hurry to get going. The bus started before Tyrone, packed down like a truck horse, had completely left the step. He went sprawling in the icy slush, his packages scattered over the immediate landscape.

Suddenly Tyrone threw back his head and laughed until the tears came. It had been a nightmare ride—but, gosh, it was funny! And the passengers had looked so satisfied when he had gone kerplunk.

He waved his hand at the general direction of the disappearing bus. "Merry Christmas, everybody!" he called after it. To this day he believes the passengers thought he was crazy!

■ But laughs aren't so easy to get now that Tyrone is a star. He is so quickly recognized—automatic deference smooths the road for him.

When they do come, he treasures them. For example, not long ago, he was working on the old Fox lot, and the custodian of the gate had never seen him.

Tyrone drove in. He was stopped. "Where do you think you're goin'?" the voice of authority stopped him. Tyrone was properly meek. "I'm to report on Stage two."

"What's your name?"

Tyrone murmured—"Power."

"Howard? Never heard o' you. Gotta pass?"

Well, it was an old situation which the public didn't believe any more. But at least, this would brighten up his day for him, Tyrone thought.

So he made profuse apologies for not having a pass. He didn't correct the gentleman on the name. This could go on for minutes on end.

But his fun was cut short. A breathless gateman who knew Tyrone rushed up. "They're waiting for you, Mr. Power. Stage two." He waved him on.

In the rear vision mirror he saw Gateman No. 1 shaking his head in consternation. And Gateman No. 2 was gesticulating wildly, probably advising his brother-worker to get up on his movies.

■ When he was working on *Alexander's Ragtime Band*, in one sequence, he as well as the extras were in khaki uniform. Tyrone had crawled up to the cat-walk which the electricians use, to get some candid camera shots.

"Hey, buddy," an electrician reminded him, "they're calling all you guys down there."

"I don't think they mean me," Tyrone replied.

"Boy, you extras sure try to get out of all the work you can. Well, it's O. K. with me, buddy, but you better not let 'em catch you with that camera."

The electrician stood guard while he took his pictures, and waved him down the ladder with the hope that the director wouldn't find out he hadn't been among those present when the extras lined up.

Tyrone thanked him. But not for the world would he let him know his identity. After all, the man was doing his good deed for the day!

And so life to Tyrone is an arena for laughs. He gets them where he can.

Laughing your way through life is a fine formula for living, Tyrone has found.

"And boy, does it get you out of jams!" he adds.

Hollywood

A FAWCETT PUBLICATION

(Reg. U. S. Pat. Off.)

'836

5¢

NOVEMBER
NSC

TRY THE
LORETTA YOUNG
"REGULAR GUY"
TEST ON YOUR
BOY FRIEND

SEE
PAGE
25

Loretta Young

TRY LORETTA YOUNG'S

"Regular Guy" TEST

Loretta Young started the whole thing on the set of her next picture, *Suez*, when she was describing one of her personal friends. "You like him because he is a regular guy," she said.

"Just what do you mean when you say 'Regular Guy?'" we asked her, and that started a discussion that eventually resulted in this questionnaire.

According to this star's way of thinking, a "regular guy" may be tall or short, fat or lean, and his age has nothing to do with his rating. BUT he has a definite policy towards clothes and sports and punctures and conversation and drinks and dish-washing, about money and movies and the morning paper.

How do your friends rate according to Miss Young's standards?

In the first place no "Regular Guy" will refuse to answer these questions, so get a pencil, settle the young man in a comfortable chair, and let him have it!

ON A DATE

1. If you are delayed, do you telephone, telling your "date" when to expect you?——

2. Do you start an evening by saying "What do you want to do?" or do you suggest something definite? (Answer first part.)——

3. Do you notice when your "date" is wearing a new dress?——

4. Think back . . . do girls always seem to be asking for cigarettes, or do you remember to wave the package at them once in a while? (Answer first part of question only.)——

5. Is your evening spoiled if your girl is not the most sensationally dressed in the party?——

6. Do you insist upon staying through the second feature, if your favorite star is on the screen and your companion doesn't want to remain?——

7. Do you think it flatters your girl to comment disparagingly on other women?——

8. Are you annoyed if the girl seems to be enjoying the conversation of other men in the party?——

9. Do you think every girl expects to be kissed goodnight?——

10. Do you know when to go home?——

IN MOMENTS OF STRESS

1. Do you scold out loud at your hard luck when you pick up a puncture?——

2. Do you speak sharply to a waiter who is giving poor service?——

3. Do you moan about having to go to the dentist, and discuss the details?——

4. Do you lend money . . . and then broadcast your generosity? Think hard, now . . . do you tell even a few people?——

5. Do you usually stop when you see a stalled car, and offer aid?——

6. Do you bring it to your hostess' attention when you burn a hole in the rug or furniture, or do you let it pass as though nothing had happened? (Answer first part of question only.)——

7. Supposing you ran out of gas late at night . . . would you try to send the girl friend home in a taxi, rather than let her wait until you've walked several miles to a gas station and returned, so that you could deliver her home yourself?——

8. Do you ever admit it was your fault when your car collides with another?——

9. Are you always talking about how broke you are?——

10. Do you ever hang up on someone who has called you on the telephone?——

AT HOME

1. Do you occasionally compliment the cook?——

2. Do you think helping around the house is unmanly?——

3. Do you try to beat everyone to the morning paper?——

4. Do you leave the paper pulled apart so that the next person has to spend minutes finding the continued line on that front page story?——

5. Do you think that messy clothes are all right, so long as only the family sees you?——

6. Do you fight with your neighbors?——

7. Do you pitch in, if need be, with the dish-washing without being asked?——

8. Do you play your radio after midnight?——

9. If you make a last minute dinner date, do you telephone home and tell the family when to expect you?——

10. Do you discuss a guest while he is under your roof with another guest?——

AT THE OFFICE

1. Do you think it sends up your stock to complain about your present job if you have had better ones in the past?——

2. Do you open or close windows without consulting the wishes of others in the office?——

3. Along about 4:30 in the afternoon, do you get all set to beat everybody else out the door the moment it is closing time?——

4. Do you think clothes important?——

5. Do you think cracking wise about the boss will win you popularity with your fellow-workers?——

6. Are you a late riser, so that you put in an appearance unshaven, with the intention of sprucing up at lunch?——

7. Do you ALWAYS have to borrow money the day before payday?——

8. Do you enjoy telling stories about your friends that begin . . . "You should have seen good old Butch the other night —he was falling-down pie-eyed and was he funny!"?——

9. Do you use a nail file in public?——

10. Do you let everyone know when you are not feeling up to par?——

AS A MAN AMONG MEN

1. Do you enjoy meeting new people?——

2. Do you read only the sports page?——

3. Do you boast of your amours?——

4. Do you play any outdoor games?——

5. Do your friends believe everything you say?——

6. Are you jealous—even in your own mind—of the success of others?——

7. Do you think you're a "born leader," and insist upon directing the activities of your associates?——

Here's a Hollywood "Quiz"—and It's Lots of Fun

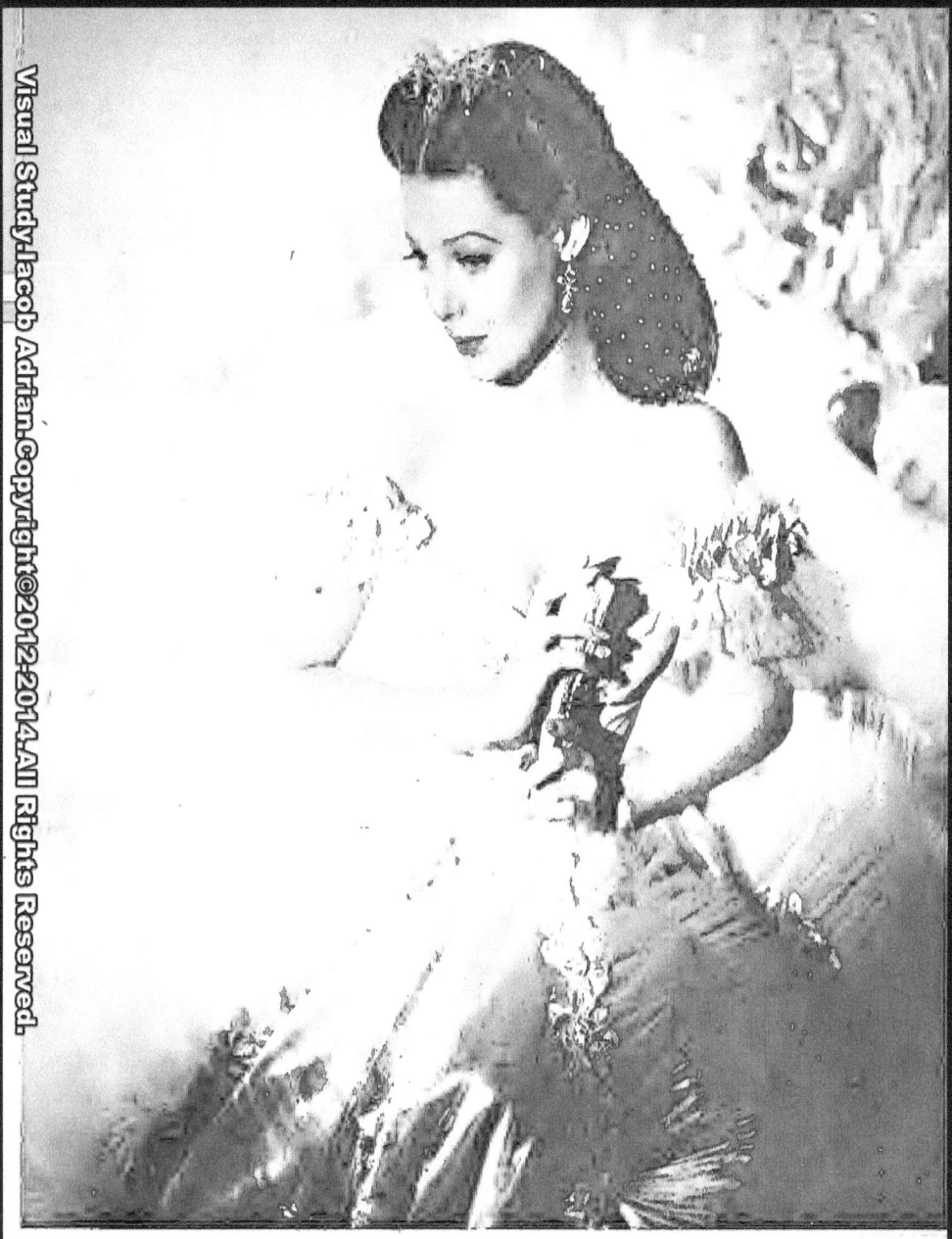

8. Do you think that you have a fatal attraction for most women?———

9. Can you let someone else tell a story all the way through without stealing a laugh or two?———

10. Are you unhappy unless conversation concerns your business?———

AT A PARTY

1. Are you outwardly reluctant when your hostess asks you to go far out of

Loretta Young, shown in one of the graceful costumes which she wears in her next film, Suez, in which she appears opposite Tyrone Power

your way home to drop someone without a car . . . and it is dreadfully late?———

2. Do you believe that the best parties are the loudest?———

3. Are you unhappy if someone else is the center of attention?———

4. Do you circulate, rather than confine yourself to a few intimate friends?———

5. Do you hold to the theory that the more drinks you consume the better time you'll have?———

6. Do you believe that off-color stories add to the gaiety of the occasion?———

7. Presuming you know the subject under argument or discussion rather intimately, does it give you satisfaction to correct others?———

Try Loretta Young's "Regular Guy" Test

8. Do you ask for drinks (or wait until they are offered)?——

9. Do you call your hostess shortly after a party and thank her for the evening?——

10. Are you always the last to leave?——

AT PLAY

1. Do you give in without argument when the majority prefers some other pastime than that which you particularly had your heart set upon doing?——

2. Are you prone to take yourself seriously if you hurt yourself—broken bones excepted on the field of sport?——

3. Do you object to taking as your partner one far your inferior in any competitive game?——

4. Do you like competitive sport?——

5. Do you hate to lose, even if you don't show it?——

6. Do you offer to concede a point that's doubtful, if it affects the score of whatever game you may be playing?——

7. Do you get an inner kick seeing some poor dope flinch when you slap his sunburned back?——

8. Do you ease up on your game just because your opponent is not near your equal?——

9. Do you like startling sports clothes?——

10. Do you discuss the other fellow's game as well as your own?——

IN YOUR OWN SWEET WAY

1. To put over a laugh, do you take a crack at another's expense?——

2. Are you strict about keeping appointments on the minute?——

3. Are you way behind in the payment of your social obligations?——

4. Would you heed a hard-luck tale on the street, rather than take the chance of passing up someone really in need of aid?——

5. Are you an I-told-you-so, by actions if not by actual words?——

6. Can you change your mind?——

7. Is it hard for you to make up your mind?——

8. Is it hard for you to change a plan?——

9. Do you like dogs?——

10. Do you hate to be pinned down by questions such as these?——

Now add up the score!

Give the young man ONE for each answer that corresponds to those listed below.

He is absolutely perfect, a jewel among males, the final flower of civilization, if his answers add up to 80.

But that is too much, almost, to expect, and if his score is 70 or better, he is a fine fellow, and deserves an admiring pat on the head.

If his score is between 60 and 70, he will have to do a lot of work before he can win a popularity contest.

If he doesn't rate better than 40, he's kidding you! Make him take the test again.

HERE ARE A REGULAR GUY'S CORRECT ANSWERS

ON A DATE

1. Yes		6. No
2. No		7. No
3. Yes		8. No
4. No		9. No
5. No		10. Yes

IN MOMENTS OF STRESS

1. No		6. Yes
2. No		7. Yes
3. No		8. Yes
4. No		9. No
5. Yes		10. No

AT HOME

1. Yes		4. No
2. No		5. No
3. Yes (everyone does and you get a score for this one on honesty!)		6. No
		7. Yes
		8. No
		9. Yes
		10. No

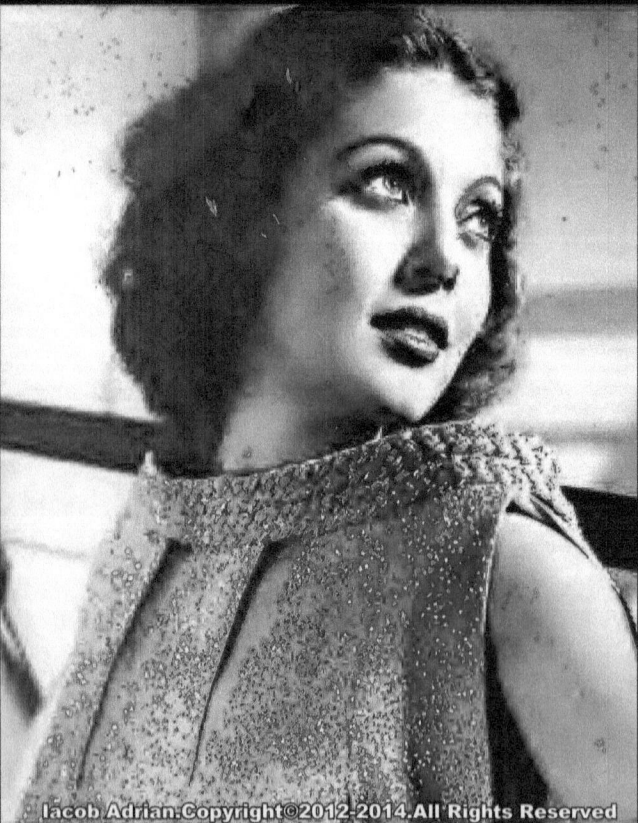

AT THE OFFICE

1. No		6. No
2. No		7. No
3. No		8. No.
4. Yes		9. No
5. No		10. No

AS A MAN AMONG MEN

1. Yes		6. No
2. No		7. No
3. No		8. No
4. Yes		9. Yes
5. Yes		10. No

AT A PARTY

1. No		6. No
2. No		7. No
3. No		8. No
4. Yes		9. Yes
5. No		10. No

AT PLAY

1. Yes		6. Yes
2. No		7. No
3. No		8. Yes
4. Yes		9. No
5. No		10. Yes

IN YOUR OWN SWEET WAY

1. No		6. Yes
2. Yes		7. No
3. No		8. No
4. Yes		9. Yes
5. No		10. No

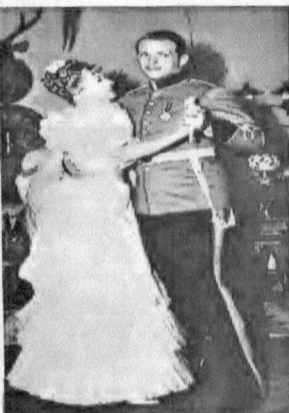

Joan Fontaine and Douglas Fairbanks, Jr., do an old-fashioned waltz for the East Indian Army Post scenes in *Gunga Din*, and seem to like it a lot

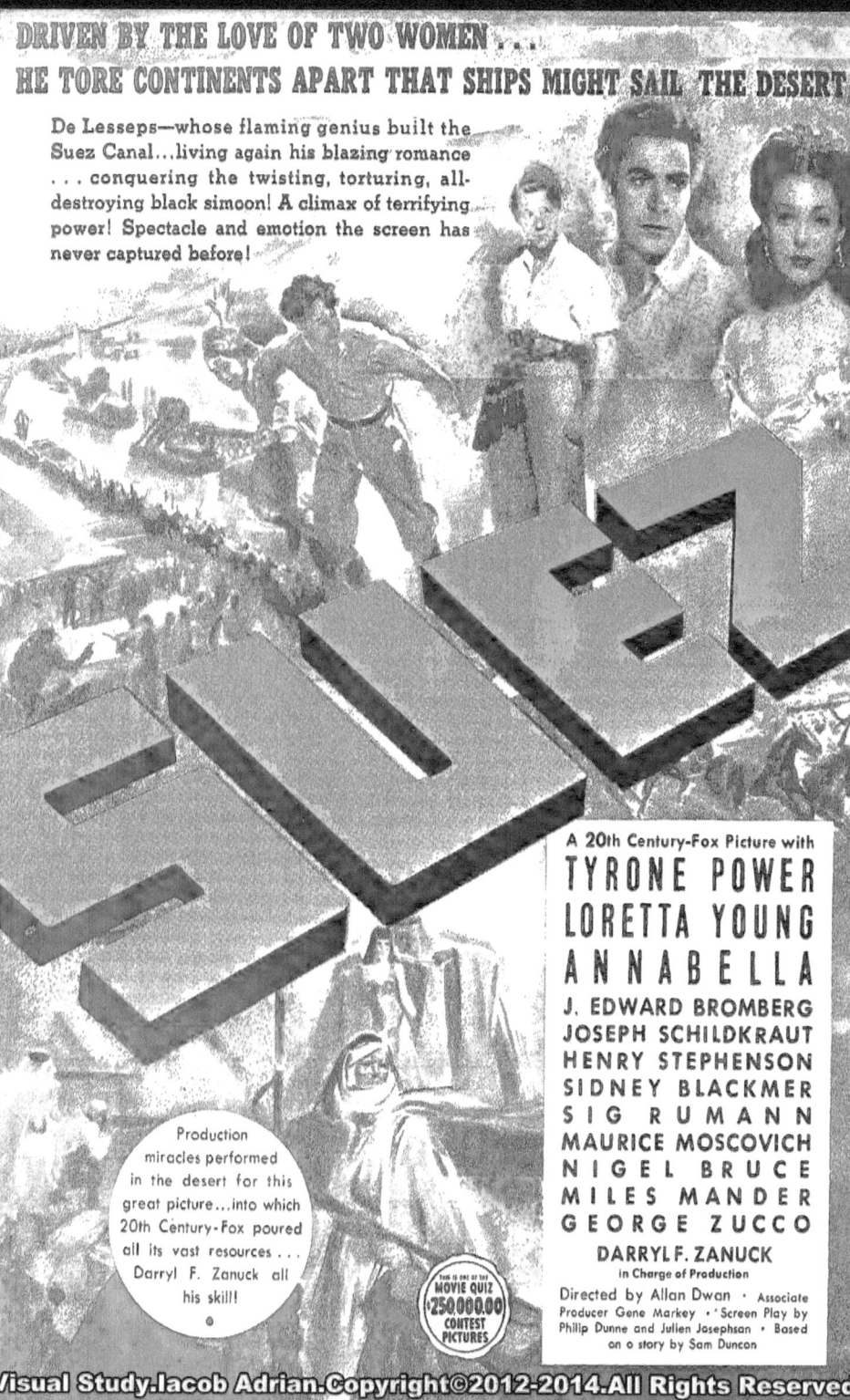

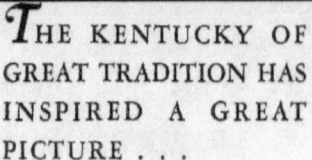

THE KENTUCKY OF
GREAT TRADITION HAS
INSPIRED A GREAT
PICTURE...
*IN ALL THE SPLENDOR
OF TECHNICOLOR!*

Proud romance...beautiful women
...chivalrous men...magnificent
thoroughbreds! The sport of kings
climaxing when the silks flash by at
Churchill Downs in the famed Kentucky Derby! All against the warm
beauty of the Blue Grass country!

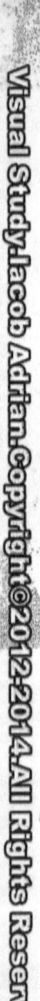
Kentucky

with

LORETTA YOUNG · **RICHARD GREENE**

and **WALTER BRENNAN** · DOUGLAS DUMBRILLE

KAREN MORLEY · MORONI OLSEN

Photographed in TECHNICOLOR

Directed by David Butler · Associate Producer Gene
Markey · Screen Play by Lamar Trotti and John Taintor Foote
From the story "The Look of Eagles" by John Taintor Foote

A 20th Century-Fox Picture

DARRYL F. ZANUCK in Charge of Production

Ask your theatre manager for KENTUCKY

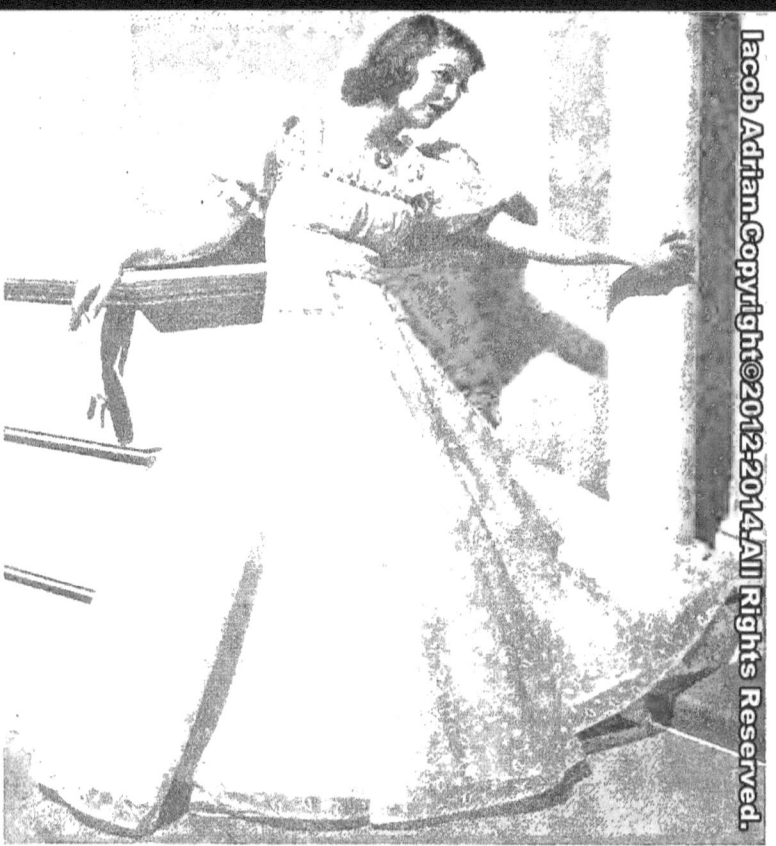

Loretta Young has her own ideas about a diet for health, and evidently it is a success for it gives her strength to go straight from her role in *Kentucky* to the leading lady's part in *Alexander Graham Bell*

Do Vegetarians Starve?

Here is one way to solve the problem of
that meatless meal appetizingly and easily

By BETTY CROCKER

I've heard people say, so frequently, that vegetarians must be half starved. Poor things, without any meat! But that's definitely not true.

"I go vegetarian ever so often," says Loretta Young, "because I think a strictly vegetable diet now and then is good for my complexion."

Well, if you saw lovely Loretta in the 20th Century-Fox technicolor picture, *Kentucky,* then you will have to admit that her delicate, rose petal complexion is sufficient proof. Even our baby stars can envy Loretta's smooth, fresh skin. If eating has anything to do with it, then there's something to be said in favor of "vegetable days."

On such occasions, Loretta sits down to this menu:

Fruit Cocktail
Spaghetti Loaf with Mushroom Sauce
Platter of Salad Greens
Snow Pudding
Butterscotch Refrigerator Cookies

The Spaghetti Loaf with Mushroom

Sauce is the meat equivalent in the meal. All the calories and vitamins have been carefully considered in this menu, and here is a well-balanced ration containing all you need.

Now, just to be sure that you fully enjoy the experience when you "go vegetarian" for a few days, I'm going to give you the kitchen tested recipes for Spaghetti Loaf with Mushroom Sauce—as well as the other dishes on Loretta Young's menu.

SPAGHETTI LOAF WITH MUSHROOM SAUCE

1⅓ cups uncooked spaghetti, broken in 1-inch pieces
1 cup milk
4 tablespoons butter
3 eggs
1 cup grated American cheese (packed)
⅔ cup soft bread crumbs (packed)
1 tablespoon chopped parsley
1 teaspoon grated onion
1 tablespoon chopped pimento
½ teaspoon salt
⅛ teaspoon pepper

Cook spaghetti until tender in 2 quarts boiling water to which 2 teaspoons salt have been added. Drain. Heat milk and butter over hot water until milk is scalded and butter melted. Pour gradually over beaten egg yolks. Add well drained spaghetti, cheese, bread crumbs, parsley, onion, pimiento and seasonings. Fold in stiffly beaten egg whites. Pour into well-buttered bread loaf pan 7¾ inches by 3½ inches across the bottom (and 3 inches deep), and bake 1 hour in a slow moderate oven, 325° F. Serve hot with Mushroom Sauce.

PLATTER OF SALAD GREENS

Arrange a variety of different salad greens on a platter, such as curly endive around the outside, inner leaves of lettuce next, then watercress sprigs, and in the center artichoke hearts. Sprinkle sliced shallots and finely minced St. Mary's herbs over all. Pass French Dressing separately.

SNOW PUDDING WITH CUSTARD SAUCE

1 tablespoon granulated gelatine
¼ cup cold water
1 cup boiling water
¾ cup sugar
¼ cup lemon juice
Grated rind of 1 lemon
Whites of 2 eggs.

Soak gelatine in cold water for 5 minutes and dissolve in boiling water. Add sugar, lemon juice and rind. Strain and set aside to cool. Stir the mixture occasionally, and when quite thick, beat with an egg beater until frothy. Add egg whites which have been beaten until stiff, and continue beating until stiff enough to hold its shape. Pile by spoonfuls on a glass dish and chill. Serve with soft custard sauce. This makes 8 servings. NOTE: This dessert may be colored pink if desired.

BUTTERSCOTCH REFRIGERATOR COOKIES

1 cup shortening (half butter for flavor)
2 cups brown sugar
2 eggs
3½ cups all-purpose flour
¼ teaspoon salt
1 teaspoon soda
1 teaspoon cream of tartar
2 tablespoons sour cream
1 teaspoon vanilla
1 cup finely-chopped nuts

Cream shortening thoroughly, add sugar gradually, and cream well. Add well-beaten eggs. Sift flour once before measuring, and sift again with salt, soda and cream of tartar. Add to creamed mixture alternately with the sour cream. Blend in vanilla. Shape dough into a roll, wrap in waxed paper, and place in refrigerator for at least 24 hours. Slice with sharp knife, place on ungreased cooky sheet (shaping with hands if necessary). Press 1 teaspoon of chopped nuts onto each slice. Bake 8 to 12 minutes (depending on thickness of cookies) in a moderately hot oven, 400° F. AMOUNT: 3 dozen cookies. NOTE: This dough may be kept in refrigerator and used as desired.

Other meat substitutes offered by Miss Young are:

CAULIFLOWER WITH HOLLANDAISE SAUCE

Steam or boil cauliflower until done, but not mushy. Serve with

HOLLANDAISE SAUCE

4 egg yolks
½ cup butter
¾ cup boiling water
¼ teaspoon salt
Few grains cayenne pepper
2 tablespoons lemon juice

Beat egg yolks until light. Add melted butter and boiling water. Cook in double boiler until mixture begins to thicken. Do not cook too long nor too hard as Hollandaise separates easily. Remove from heat and add seasonings and lemon juice.

CORN AND TOMATOES AU GRATIN

1 No. 2 can whole kernel corn (2½ cups)
1 No. 2 can tomatoes (2½ cups)
1 small green pepper, chopped
1 cup coarse cracker crumbs
1½ teaspoons salt
1-16 teaspoon pepper
1 teaspoon sugar
3 tablespoons melted butter
⅓ cup grated American cheese
2 tablespoons butter

Combine corn, tomatoes, green pepper, ½ cup of the cracker crumbs, salt, pepper, sugar and melted butter. Pour into a large shallow buttered baking dish (10x6 inches and 2 inches deep). Sprinkle cheese and remaining ½ cup cracker crumbs over top and dot with butter. Bake 30 minutes in a moderately hot oven, 400° F. AMOUNT: 8 to 10 servings.

Now, if you wish to discover for yourself whether vegetarians fare so badly, try this menu. It's Loretta's favorite for Friday, which is strictly meatless in her family.

And for you who still think a meal isn't worth sitting down to unless it contains meat, I'm going to add a delicious recipe for Mock Duck which I have found most successful.

MOCK DUCK

Buy a shoulder of lamb or mutton from the forequarter (about 5 pounds). Have your butcher leave the foreleg on, and cut off about four inches below the knee, to form the head and neck of duck. Have the shoulder boned, and mold and sew in the shape of body of duck—leaving a hollow for stuffing. The foreleg should stand up to give effect of neck and head. The leg bone may be split an inch to form a mouth. Bits of bone make natural looking eyes. Remove a few of the stitches and fill the hollow with Peanut Stuffing. Resew or fasten securely with skewers. Rub Mock Duck with fat, sprinkle with flour, salt and pepper, and roast in a hot oven 20 minutes, turning so that all sides become browned. TIME: Roast uncovered for 20 minutes, then reduce heat, cover and allow 20 to 25 minutes for each pound. TEMPERATURE: 475° F., very hot oven, for first 20 minutes, reducing heat to 350° F., moderate oven, to finish baking.

PEANUT STUFFING

1 cup cracker or bread crumbs
¾ cup shelled peanuts, coarsely ground
½ cup milk (or enough to moisten)
1 tablespoon melted butter
½ teaspoon salt
⅛ teaspoon pepper
Few drops onion juice
Few grains cayenne pepper

Mix all ingredients in order given. Use for stuffing Mock Duck. NOTE: This amount of stuffing will probably not all go into the duck, but may be baked separately in the pan.

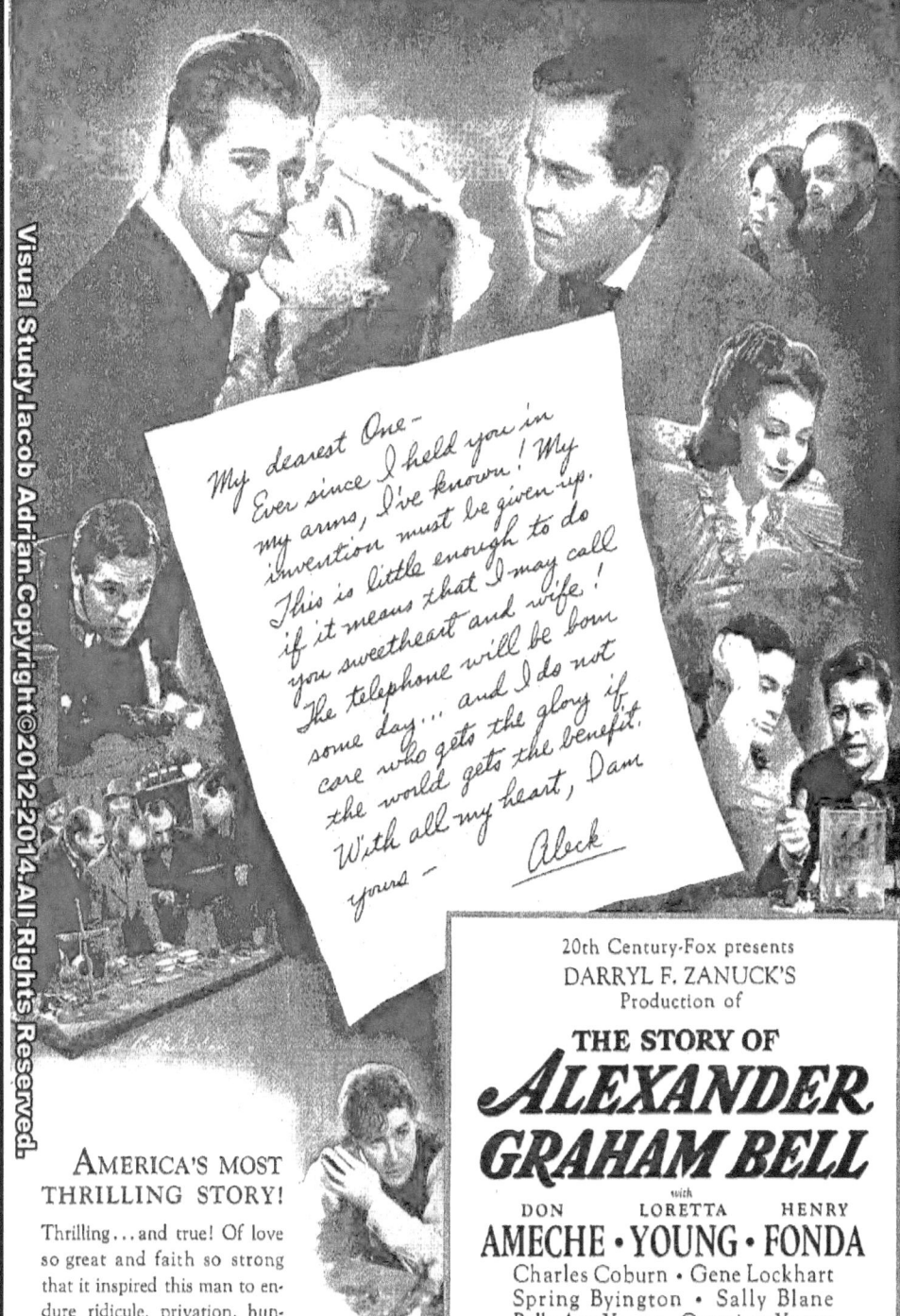

My dearest One —
Ever since I held you in
my arms, I've known! My
invention must be given up,
This is little enough to do
if it means that I may call
you sweetheart and wife!
The telephone will be born
some day ... and I do not
care who gets the glory if
the world gets the benefit.
With all my heart, I am
yours —
       Aleck

20th Century-Fox presents
DARRYL F. ZANUCK'S
Production of

THE STORY OF

ALEXANDER GRAHAM BELL

with

DON	LORETTA	HENRY
AMECHE •	**YOUNG** •	**FONDA**

Charles Coburn • Gene Lockhart
Spring Byington • Sally Blane
Polly Ann Young • Georgiana Young
A Cosmopolitan Production
Directed by Irving Cummings • Associate Producer
Kenneth Macgowan • Screen Play by Lamar Trotti
Original story by Ray Harris

AMERICA'S MOST THRILLING STORY!

Thrilling ... and true! Of love
so great and faith so strong
that it inspired this man to en-
dure ridicule, privation, hunger ... to achieve the miracle
of wings for the human voice!

Post-Graduate Course

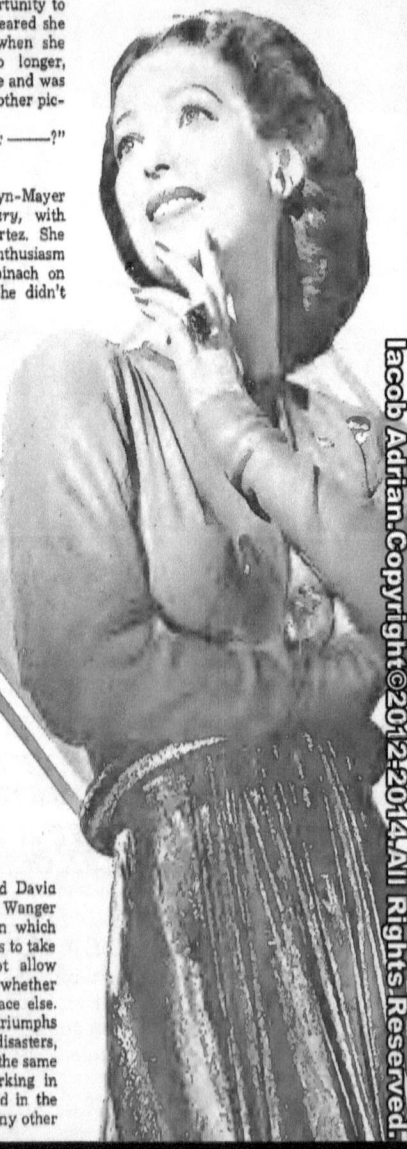

Not so very long ago Loretta Young fell in love with a script. She read it, thought it perfect, decided that it would be her greatest opportunity. She felt that life wouldn't be worth while unless she could do it. She was under contract to Warner Brothers at the time. The powers-that-be told her that she could have the role—probably.

As the weeks passed, the role grew more and more important to her. The picture became very near and dear to her. She alternately rejoiced at the opportunity to do it and fretted, worried and feared she wouldn't get the part. Just when she could stand the suspense no longer, Loretta was called into the office and was told that she was going to do another picture at another studio first.

"But will I get back in time for ———?" she asked breathlessly.

"Of course," was the answer.

So she went to Metro-Goldwyn-Mayer and worked in *Midnight Mary*, with Franchot Tone and Ricardo Cortez. She went at her role with all the enthusiasm and vigor of a child eating spinach on pain of getting no dessert if she didn't polish her plate. And, while *Midnight Mary* was being directed merrily by William Wellman, up popped the picture of pictures at Warner Brothers.

Somebody else got the role.

Loretta had a good cry for herself. She was sure she was abused by fate, kicked around by the front office, the victim of luck hard enough to cut diamonds. Days went into weeks, weeks into months, and still she worried because she hadn't been able to do that part—until the picture was previewed and released. It turned out to be one of the finest floperoos Hollywood had turned out in many moons.

On the other hand, the picture she hadn't wanted to do, particularly—*Midnight Mary*—was a hit.

"And so," she said as she relaxed between scenes of *Eternally Yours*, which she and David Niven are making for Walter Wanger productions, "I learned a lesson which has always stuck with me. That's to take everything in your stride, not allow yourself to be disappointed, whether you're in Hollywood or any place else. For Hollywood, with its petty triumphs and its big ones, its problems, disasters, laughs and heartaches, is much the same as any other community. Working in pictures is essentially work, and in the main not much different from any other

Hollywood has many lessons to teach. The most important is "Never stop learning!" according to Loretta

By EDWARD CHURCHILL

kind of employment." Loretta confesses that she's learned a great deal in the twelve years she's been featured and starred in motion pictures, dating from her first big role in the Lon Chaney picture, *Laugh, Clown, Laugh*. She was fourteen then. She had been before the cameras off and on since her pre-school days, shortly after her mother and her sisters, Sally Blaine and Polly Ann Young, arrived in Hollywood from Salt Lake City.

We were discussing the tendency to gossip, a vicious little pastime which is all too common, when she told of one of the most embarrassing experiences of her early career—an experience that taught her a lesson she never will forget.

"I heard a story about a writer," she recalled. "I got it fourth or fifth hand. I passed it along, adding a few little flourishes to get 'ohs' and 'ahs' from my audience. I didn't stop to think that such gossip might not be true, and that those who had passed it on to me might have elaborated a bit, even as I had."

The gossip rebounded. Her telephone rang. It was the writer, a man famous in Hollywood.

"I hear you've been telling a story about me," he said, and repeated the tale Loretta had told. "What makes you think it's true?"

Loretta paused to consider this and remembered that, while it had been given to her by a woman of unimpeachable character, that woman in turn might have picked it up from someone who had viciously fabricated the whole thing.

"I don't know," she faltered.

"Well, it isn't true," the writer said. And, in a very nice way, he pointed out where the story had originated, why, how it had grown, had become unkind and even dangerous to his career and reputation. She apologized. The writer understood, and they became fast friends.

"That was an embarrassing, hard-to-take and much deserved lesson," she pointed out. "Gossip is without excuse in Hollywood or any place else. And keep this in mind—it isn't the true things people say about you that hurt. It's the falsehoods which one passes on about [Continued on page 68]

[Continued on page 68]

Loretta Young in one of the spectacular gowns from her next film, *Eternally Yours*

Have Some Studio Food!

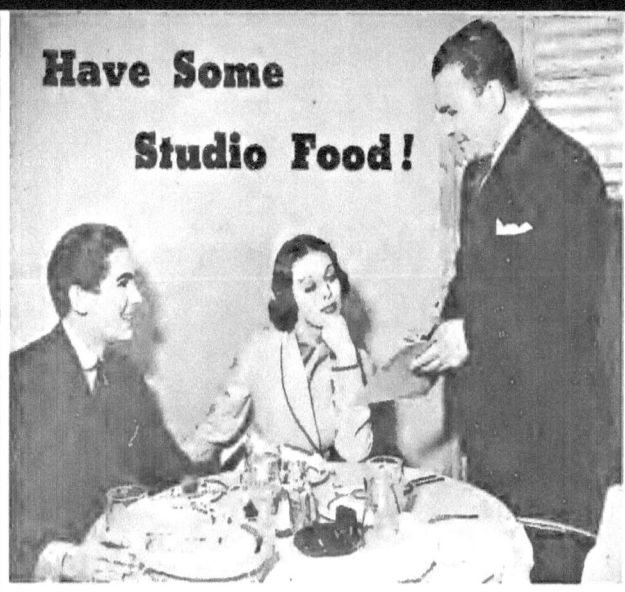

Tyrone Power and Loretta Young are two of the hundreds of stars and studio workers for whom Nick Janios prepares delicious, unusual dishes

By BETTY CROCKER

It's probably the only famous restaurant in the world where they have police to keep out the public, but that isn't all that makes the Cafe de Paris unique. Twentieth Century-Fox operates the Cafe at a loss to feed its stars in the grand manner, and the gentleman in charge of this important function is Nick Janios.

Nick knows more celebrities by their first names than anyone else, but what is more important at the moment, he knows exactly what they eat and what cooking recipes they cherish.

He watches Shirley Temple's diet with as much care as her mother does. Shirley loves to filch a huge, fattening pastry, but Nick sees to it that she eats sensibly. He enlisted Alice Faye in "selling" her on spinach and carrots. He baked a cake for Hedy Lamarr's birthday that drew as much attention as the glamour girl herself, which is certainly something!

Nick sends his chief chef, Alfred Uhlrich, on an annual tour to bring back word of new delicacies, and until the war, Uhlrich visited the capitals of Europe every year. After his return, the Cafe is a busy spot for days as they try out new dishes in the big kitchens.

Now for some of the favorite recipes of the stars, gathered from the confidential portfolio of the Cafe de Paris. Let's start with a delicious meat dish favored by Alice Faye:

ALICE FAYE'S "TALLARNEE"

2 heaping cupfuls uncooked noodles
1 pound of round steak, ground
1 can of tomato sauce (or soup)
1 can of corn
1 can of ripe olives
1 cupful grated cheese
1 medium onion, chopped
2 heaping tablespoons butter
1 cupful water

Mince and fry onion in butter until brown. Add meat. Stir and cook until browned. Add tomato sauce and a cupful of water. Add noodles; stir and cook until the noodles are tender. More water may have to be added to keep mixture moist. Salt to taste. Add corn and olives. Pour into large buttered casserole. Sprinkle with cheese. Cook 45 minutes in a 350 degree oven.

RICHARD GREENE'S "RUBY PIE"

Wash 2½ cups cranberries
1¾ cupfuls sugar
1½ cups cold water

Cook in covered saucepan until the berries stop popping. Put ⅓ of the berries into a deep, well-greased pie plate. Add a layer of sliced bananas. Continue with alternate layers of cranberries and bananas. Cover fruit with pie crust, fitting the pastry closely around the edge of the dish. Slash the crust and bake in a hot oven about 25 minutes, until the crust is well browned.

DON AMECHE'S CREAMED SHRIMP WITH RICE

2 pints shrimp
1 tablespoon tomato catsup
2 tablespoons butter
½ grated onion
½ cup boiled rice
1 gill cream
Salt and pepper to taste

Put the butter in the pan . . . when melted stir in the onion, then the rice, pepper and salt. Add the cream, shrimps and catsup. Stir until very hot. Let it simmer for five minutes and serve on toast. Serve from a chafing dish at the table.

SHIRLEY TEMPLE'S HADDON HALL GINGERBREAD

½ cup shortening
2 tablespoons sugar
1 egg
1 cup dark molasses
2¼ cups all purpose flour
1 teaspoon soda

½ teaspoon salt
1 teaspoon ginger
1 teaspoon cinnamon
1 cup boiling water

Cream shortening and add the sugar, 1 tablespoon at a time. Add the well beaten egg and the molasses. Sift flour once before measuring. Sift flour, soda, salt, ginger and cinnamon together and add alternately with the boiling water and mix well. Pour into a deep eight-inch square pan lined with greased paper and bake for 45 minutes in a moderate slow oven.

Beautiful Ballerina

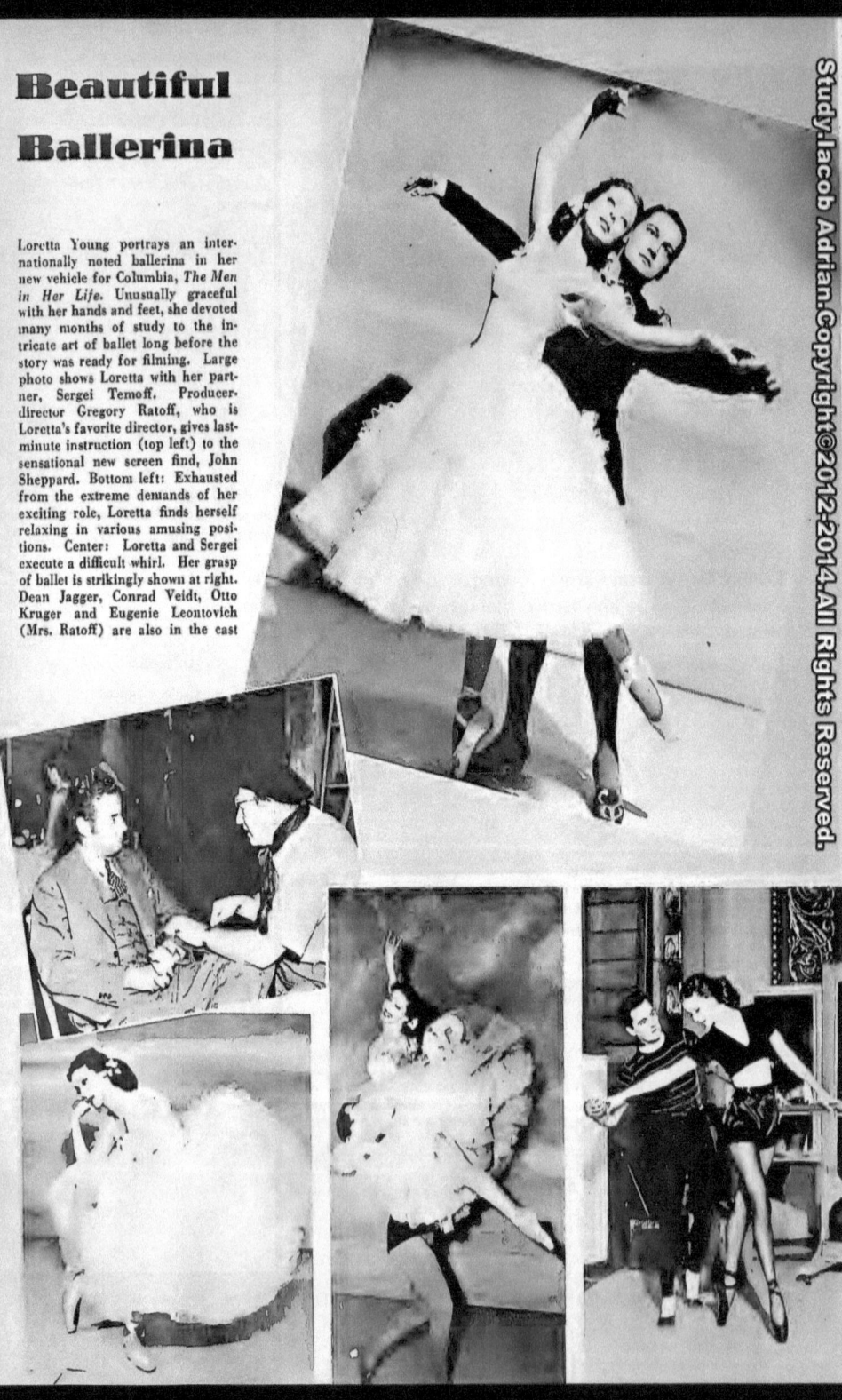

Loretta Young portrays an internationally noted ballerina in her new vehicle for Columbia, *The Men in Her Life*. Unusually graceful with her hands and feet, she devoted many months of study to the intricate art of ballet long before the story was ready for filming. Large photo shows Loretta with her partner, Sergei Temoff. Producer-director Gregory Ratoff, who is Loretta's favorite director, gives last-minute instruction (top left) to the sensational new screen find, John Sheppard. Bottom left: Exhausted from the extreme demands of her exciting role, Loretta finds herself relaxing in various amusing positions. Center: Loretta and Sergei execute a difficult whirl. Her grasp of ballet is strikingly shown at right. Dean Jagger, Conrad Veidt, Otto Kruger and Eugenie Leontovich (Mrs. Ratoff) are also in the cast

HOLLYWOOD NEWSREEL

By ERSKINE JOHNSON

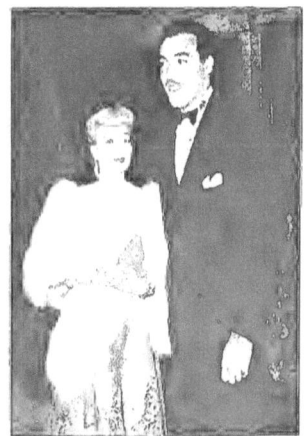

Cesar Romero has been Ann Sothern's constant escort since the separation of Ann and her husband, Roger Pryor.

■ Jane Withers finds the cost of romance is pretty heavy. She has to have three pairs of shoes in readiness every evening. When she goes out with Buddy Pepper, Boy Friend No. 1, she wears low heels because Buddy is short. When she steps out with Freddie Bartholomew, Boy Friend No. 2, she wears medium heels. He's medium height. And when Robert Cornell takes her dancing, she wears high heels—to keep his chin from doing a rhumba on her head.

■ Alice Faye is going to have a three million dollar baby—the highest priced infant in the history of Hollywood. Alice's studio, 20th Century-Fox, had scheduled her for three pictures during the coming year that would cost two million dollars and would gross, the studio thinks, at least five million. But the stork intervened. Alice will desert the screen for a year and the studio is out three million dollars.

■ When can you do the Can Can and when can't you. Even the Hays office censors don't know.

Three years ago Claudette Colbert did the famous French dance in the picture *Zaza*. And the movie censors cut out most of the scene. Now red-haired Rita Hayworth will do the same notorious dance in her new picture, *Eadie Was a Lady*, and the Hays office has approved the script.

■ Although she's free legally, Marjorie Weaver can not consider another marriage before next April unless she breaks her promise. She divorced Lieut. Kenneth Schacht of the U.S. Navy in Reno. But under the law she could not divorce him without his consent because he's stationed outside the United States in Uncle Sam's armed forces. He gave his consent to the divorce when Marjorie promised she would not become engaged to anyone else until he returns to Hollywood from the Philippines next April. It might mean a reconciliation.

■ A producer at Paramount became upset the other day because the noise of a piano came through to his office during a story conference. The producer ordered an office boy to "tell that piano tuner to cut it out." The office boy located the source of the nuisance and told the man at the baby grand that he was making too much noise. The man stopped playing. The man at the piano happened to be Irving Berlin, who was composing tunes for his new picture, *Holiday Inn*.

■ There's a feud behind every telephone pole in Hollywood, with Greta Garbo and Joan Blondell providing the best and

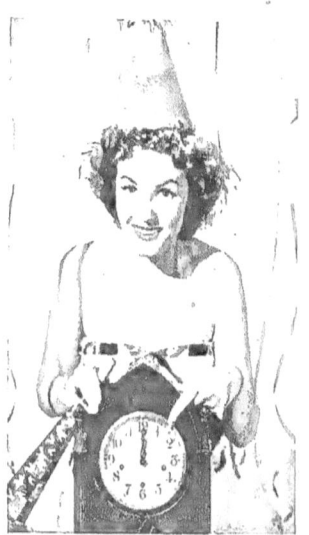

Paramount's attractive Eleanor Stewart gives a preview on how she will celebrate come midnight December 31st

latest. They're disagreeing over hair—the long and the short of it. Garbo, who recently cut her famous long bob for her latest film, is on the short end of the argument. Miss Blondell, ordered by the studio to acquire a similar bob for her role in *Lady For a Night*, refused on the grounds that it's impractical and unattractive. "How can you be a lady for even one night," asks Joan, "with a haircut like that?"

■ Success In Reverse: As m. c. at the Tower theater in Kansas City, Jack Carson presided over many amateur night shows. The other day he received a letter from one of his contest winners. It was written from a cell in California's San Quentin prison.

■ Joan Fontaine and hubby Brian Aherne's trip East was supposed to be a vacation, but Joan spent some time un-

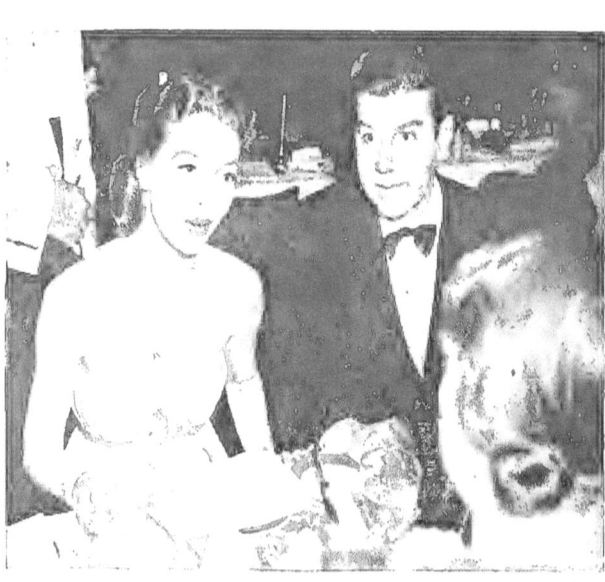

Loretta Young and her wide-eyed husband, Tom Lewis, are shown at Joan Bennett's party at Ciro's after the premiere of *Sundown*. Having completed work on Columbia's *The Men in Her Life*, Loretta is currently working on *Bedtime Story*

THE LIFE AND LOVES OF AN EXCITING WOMAN!

DAVID... her pulses throbbed...

ROSING... she learned from him...

ROGER... her heart glowed...

VICTOR... sheer devotion!

Loretta Young

IN

THE MEN IN HER LIFE

with

CONRAD VEIDT • DEAN JAGGER

JOHN SHEPPERD • OTTO KRUGER • EUGENIE LEONTOVICH

Based on a novel by Lady Eleanor Smith • Screen play by Frederick Kohner, Michael Wilson, Paul Trivers
Directed by GREGORY RATOFF • A GREGORY RATOFF PRODUCTION • A COLUMBIA PICTURE

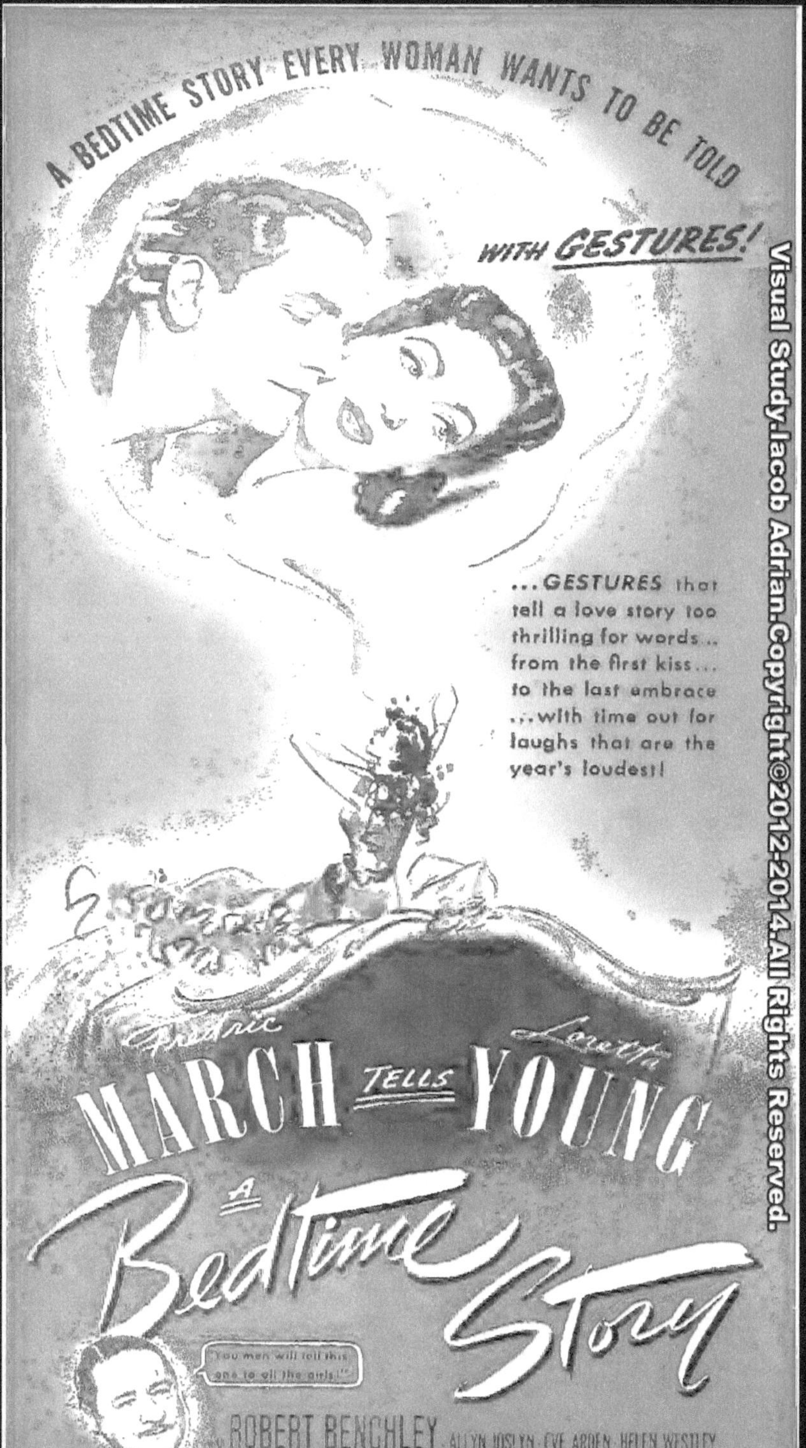

A BEDTIME STORY EVERY WOMAN WANTS TO BE TOLD

WITH *GESTURES!*

...*GESTURES* that
tell a love story too
thrilling for words...
from the first kiss...
to the last embrace
...with time out for
laughs that are the
year's loudest!

Fredric
MARCH *TELLS* Loretta
YOUNG

A
Bedtime
Story

"You men will tell this
one to all the girls!"

ROBERT BENCHLEY AND ALLYN JOSLYN · EVE ARDEN · HELEN WESTLEY

Screen play by Richard Kollmar · Story by Horace Jackson and Grant Garrett · Produced by B. P. SCHULBERG

Directed by ALEXANDER HALL · A COLUMBIA PICTURE

"What Men Have Taught Me"
— Loretta Young

Men in my life have taught me many things.

They didn't know that they were teaching me things, these men whom I have known during my long movie life; and it is a long life, although I'm only 29 years old. You see, I began in pictures when I was just four years old.

I think that some of them will be rather surprised to find themselves listed among my teachers. I hope that they will not mind.

I have learned things from men like Clark Gable, Ronald Colman, Warner Baxter, Franchot Tone, Robert Taylor, Tyrone Power, Douglas Fairbanks, Jr., Spencer Tracy, George Brent and James Cagney. The man who taught me my first and perhaps most important lesson was one who is no longer here—Lon Chaney.

I was 15 years old, struggling with one of my first really important parts in *Laugh, Clown, Laugh*.

I was scared to death. There I was, a mere youngster, trying to handle a grown-up role, painfully conscious that this was my big chance, realizing that, after all, I didn't know a great deal about acting.

Herbert Brenon was directing, and, to my young mind, he was being terribly harsh and unreasonable about it. Everything I did was wrong. Every time I tried, it was worse.

At last, Brenon shouted at me that I was terrible. I knew that I was, and that didn't make it any better. I burst into tears and rushed off the set.

Lon Chaney followed me. He waited until I had my cry out, and then he began to talk to me, very calmly.

"Listen, youngster, this is a hard game. Everyone is driving someone else, or if he isn't driving someone else, he's driving himself. Brenon knows that you can do it, or you wouldn't be here. Now, come on—let's try again."

It sounds so simple, but that little speech did the most amazing things to me. I understood, without any more words, what he meant. I turned and walked back on the set, and tried again—tried harder than I ever had in my life, but this time I wasn't thinking about myself. I was thinking about what I had to do.

In the back of my mind, I said to myself: "Of course, I can do it. Brenon knows it. Chaney said so. And I know it. This was what Brenon meant all the time, when he was scolding me. It was just his way of getting results."

The scene was a success, because I stopped being antagonistic and resentful, and worked with the director instead of against him.

That was my first big lesson—that in life, just as in the acting profession, no one can hope for real and lasting success by standing apart and aloof; that teamwork is what counts.

Because Lon Chaney taught me that so long ago, I have been able to learn from other men in my movie life. So many of them have, perhaps unconsciously, taught me things that have helped.

There was Warner Baxter, charming, master of any situation, unruffled under any circumstances. His self-control was an inspiration to that calmness and poise which one needs in life as well as in show business.

Clark Gable is a living example of naturalness and good fellowship. There is no one I know more "regular" than Clark. In his presence, one is ashamed of any selfish impulse. I think I know why Clark has so many real friends. It's because he is such a true friend himself, because he likes people, because his manner says so. If I ever felt myself getting "selfish," I should think of Clark Gable and change my ways in a hurry.

For dignity and reserve, there are few like Ronald Colman. Yet he never makes one feel ill at ease, for rudeness and thoughtlessness are no part of his make-up. He has the rare knack of seeming aloof without actually being so, which wins both respect and friendship. In him is the

when they become successful. If I ever feel myself going highbrow and haughty, I think of such men as Bob Taylor.

The only bashful leading man I ever had was Tyrone Power. However, that was in *Ladies in Love*, one of his first pictures. He got over his shyness as time went on. I have known him for years and we have made many pictures together, yet he has never lost the appealing quality that hints at just a little timidity underlying everything. I think that it would be well if all of us could keep a little bashfulness; it is a wholesome balance against too much cocksureness and vanity.

Douglas Fairbanks, Jr., is a confirmed romanticist, like his father; a romanticist in the sense that he is forever searching for interesting people. That's good, for in a search for an ideal, one comes slowly to be like the ideal. Doug impresses on you the importance of high standards in measuring people and at the same time accepting all for what they are. He looks for the good, the vital and the interesting qualities, and in doing that, helps develop those qualities in himself.

[*Continued on page 56*]

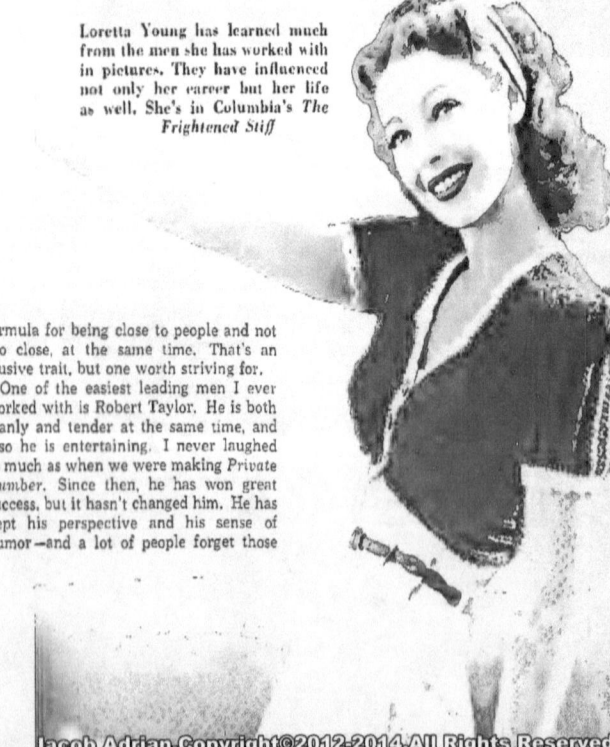

Loretta Young has learned much from the men she has worked with in pictures. They have influenced not only her career but her life as well. She's in Columbia's *The Frightened Stiff*

formula for being close to people and not too close, at the same time. That's an elusive trait, but one worth striving for.

One of the easiest leading men I ever worked with is Robert Taylor. He is both manly and tender at the same time, and also he is entertaining. I never laughed so much as when we were making *Private Number*. Since then, he has won great success, but it hasn't changed him. He has kept his perspective and his sense of humor—and a lot of people forget those remember me, I want them to say that I've brought some happiness into the lives of those who have seen me on the screen. And I want them to say that I've done the best I've known how."

That perhaps is the keynote to the entire personality of Don Ameche. He has a keen sense of responsibility and he is not one to rationalize or excuse his own shortcomings. He never shirks. He does his job.

Don leads a quiet, family life. He has four sons—Donny, nine; Ronny, six and a half; Tommy, three, and Lonny, two. The oldest one has just reached the age where he enjoys following Dad around the golf course.

"Like every working man, I don't get to see the children nearly enough," he declares. "When I am on a picture, I leave before they're up, and I get home long after they're in bed. I try to make up for it on Sundays."

The Ameches are considered in Hollywood among the most happily marrieds. Don met Honore, his wife, when they were both youngsters, attending school in Dubuque, Iowa.

Six years later they met by accident in Chicago. Don's theater apprenticeship was behind him. He had had the "bean course" —which means that when he was trying to grab a foothold in New York, he subsisted mainly on beans. He had had a few fairly good parts on which he had cut his acting teeth.

At the time of their Chicago meeting, Don was well established on the radio as the star of the "First Nighter" programs. He took Honore dancing, and while dancing, he told her that he was going to marry her. Just like that. Honore thought he was kidding.

Their courtship was conducted at long range, since Honore lived in Dubuque and it's quite a stretch from Chicago. One night he telephoned her not to go to bed—that he had a surprise for her.

At four o'clock in the morning he arrived—grease-smeared from changing tires—and half a minute later, Honore had an engagement ring on her finger.

That romantic flavor to their marriage has lasted. Honore goes wherever Don goes. If impulsively he decides to fly up to San Francisco, or to drive down to Palm Springs or up to Arrowhead in the middle of the night, she isn't the wife to dissuade him.

But such excursions, of course, are between-picture episodes. When he is working, he has time for nothing else.

Like the rest of Hollywood, he is in service for the duration, and his talents are at the disposal of his country. That means that he will entertain the boys in camps, play in benefits, go on bond-selling tours at any time he is called to do so.

Through the years Don has been on the screen, there has never been a waning period in his popularity. Year by year, his fan mail grows. Year by year his value to his studio has increased. As the options on his contract have come up, Twentieth Century-Fox has lifted them. The studio has just picked up another one on him.

If life has pulled up an easy chair for Don Ameche, he hasn't been satisfied to just sit in it.

He tries every day to re-earn the right to occupy it! ■

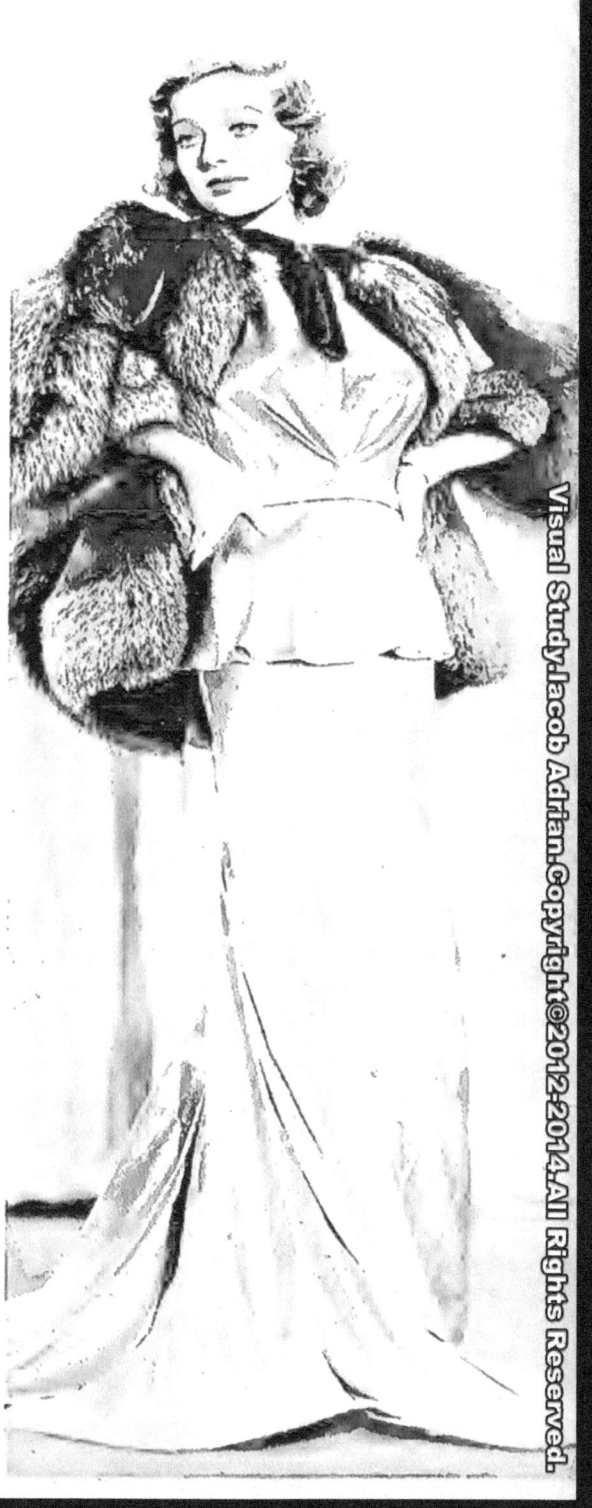

Bibliographic sources :

Hollywood (1934-1943)
Publisher: Hollywood Magazine, inc. ; Fawcett Publications, inc.

The New Movie Magazine (1929-1935)
Publisher: Tower Magazines, inc.

This documentary study use,
combined in various proportions,
elements from the following categories,
forms and subsets :
- fair use
- documentary
- documentary photography
- feature
- journalism
- arts journalism
- visual journalism
- photojournalism
- celebrity photography
in order to :
- employ material as the object of cultural critique ,
- quote to illustrate an argument or point ,
- use material in historical sequence,
providing independent opinion,
using photos, press articles, advertisements,
opinions of fans etc. ...